"This book beautifully, and in some spaces hauntingly, weaves together the story of the unhoused while providing crucial racial analysis that did my soul so much good to read. I think this book deserves a space in classrooms and libraries all across this country."

Robert Monson, codirector of Enfleshed, writer, and podcaster

"*All God's Children* isn't a feel-good, let's-all-get-along book, but it's absolutely about love—the kind of love that confronts injustice at every turn. I'm so thankful for Lester and this heartfelt, challenging book."

Marla Taviano, author of *unbelieve* and *jaded*

"Terence is one of my favorite voices on the topics of justice and faith. For him, they're inseparable. . . . This book is spiritual formation literature at its finest."

Brandy Wallner, spiritual writer

"Lester weaves faithful insights and historical context alongside his own personal history and helps us break down the ill-conceived barriers that keep us from living out the solidarity to which God calls us."

Chad Wright-Pittman, associate pastor for care and outreach at First Presbyterian Church of Anderson

"If you desire to participate in the hard and necessary work of confronting what has been harmful to so many of your brothers and sisters in the body of Christ, this book is for you."

Jerome D. Lubbe, CEO of Thrive Humancare

"*All God's Children* is a courageous conversation, an honest assessment of reality, and a step toward a future that honors God's kingdom."

Camille Hernandez, public educator, abolitionist, and author of *The Hero and the Whore*

"Terence Lester shares some of his own stories—as well as some of those he has learned from in his many years of allyship and advocacy with and for the unhoused—in demonstrating that true belonging occurs when we honor the testimony of all who have been crafted in the image of God."

R. G. A. "Trey" Ferguson III, founding president of RFX Ministries

"This book will change you, challenge you, or affirm the work you are already doing as holy work that must be continued. *All God's Children* is a book I will be returning to and sharing with everyone I know."

Monica DiCristina, therapist, writer, and host of the *Still Becoming* podcast

"I love books that tell a compelling story and challenge me to think. *All God's Children* certainly accomplishes both objectives. Terence's writing on racial solidarity is powerful because he shares from a place of expertise, experience, and empathy."

Ezra Byer, creator of The Monday Christian and author of *Walking with a Limp*

FOREWORD BY DANIEL HILL

TERENCE LESTER

ALL GOD'S CHILDREN

HOW CONFRONTING BURIED HISTORY CAN BUILD RACIAL SOLIDARITY

ivp

An imprint of InterVarsity Press
Downers Grove, Illinois

InterVarsity Press
P.O. Box 1400 | Downers Grove, IL 60515-1426
ivpress.com | email@ivpress.com

InterVarsity Press® is the publishing division of InterVarsity Christian Fellowship/USA®. For more information, visit intervarsity.org.

All Scripture quotations, unless otherwise indicated, are taken from The Holy Bible, New International Version®, NIV®. Copyright © 1973, 1978, 1984, 2011 by Biblica, Inc.™ Used by permission of Zondervan. All rights reserved worldwide. www.zondervan.com. The "NIV" and "New International Version" are trademarks registered in the United States Patent and Trademark Office by Biblica, Inc.™

Author is represented by Illuminate Literary Agency, www.illuminateliterary.com.

While any stories in this book are true, some names and identifying information may have been changed to protect the privacy of individuals.

The publisher cannot verify the accuracy or functionality of website URLs used in this book beyond the date of publication.

Cover design: David Fassett
Interior design: Daniel van Loon

ISBN 978-1-5140-0595-8 (print) | ISBN 978-1-5140-0596-5 (digital)

Printed in the United States of America ∞

Library of Congress Cataloging-in-Publication Data
Names: Lester, Terence, author.
Title: All God's children : how confronting buried history can build racial
    solidarity / Terence Lester ; foreword by Daniel Hill.
Other titles: How confronting buried history can build racial solidarity
Description: Downers Grove, IL : InterVarsity Press, 2023. | Includes
    bibliographical references.
Identifiers: LCCN 2022059538 (print) | LCCN 2022059539 (ebook) | ISBN
    9781514005958 (print) | ISBN 9781514005965 (digital)
Subjects: LCSH: Racism–United States. | African Americans–Social
    conditions. | Race relations–Religious aspects–Christianity. | Church
    and social problems–United States. | United States–Race
    relations–History.
Classification: LCC E185.615 .L476 2023 (print) | LCC E185.615 (ebook) |
    DDC 305.896/073–dc23/eng/20230217
LC record available at https://lccn.loc.gov/2022059538
LC ebook record available at https://lccn.loc.gov/2022059539

29 28 27 26 25 24 23 | 12 11 10 9 8 7 6 5 4 3 2 1

I **dedicate this book** *to my family—Cecilia, Zion, and Terence II. Thank you for being my church and safe space while I was going through the hardest moments of my life. I also dedicate this book to my biological father, Tyrone Lester, who has become a good friend in my adult years.*

I **dedicate this book** *to anyone who has ever experienced any form of racism, exclusion, or mistreatment for simply having Black or Brown skin.*

Last, I dedicate this book *to those who genuinely want to learn, grow, and make this world a better place, not through mere talk but through action.*

In memory of *the late Herman S. Lester Sr.*

CONTENTS

Foreword by Daniel Hill   1

Introduction: Everyone Has a Story   5

1 A Past I Could Not Touch   25

2 A History Few Wanted to Understand   46

3 God Is Justice   65

4 Confronting Buried History   86

5 Unpacking Biases   106

6 Engaging Differences   123

7 Engage Your Community   142

8 Practice Proximity   155

9 Sit at Another's Table   171

10 Break the Silence   187

Conclusion: Be the Solution   202

Afterword by Vonnetta L. West   209

Acknowledgments   213

Appendix: Further Educational Material   217

Notes   219

FOREWORD

As I joyfully read through Terence Lester's amazing book *All God's Children*, I realized this was exactly the resource we need for the wilderness season we find ourselves in. I first heard the term *wilderness* to describe the current season of our nation from author and historian Jemar Tisby. I think it's an idea we should all grapple with, especially as we get ready to read this important book.

Tisby suggested that the wilderness is a familiar theme through the pages of Scripture. (Commentators say that there are as many as three hundred wilderness passages.) Lester understands that while there are times that a biblical experience in the wilderness could be described as uplifting, we more often find wilderness experiences described as periods of disorientation, confusion, and even distress. There are so many different reasons why people end up in the wilderness. Moses was running for his life. Jacob was waiting to see if his brother wanted revenge. Elijah was depressed and depleted.

The nation of Israel was learning critical lessons on their way to the Promised Land. But no matter how they may have gotten there, what they needed next remained true for all of them.

In the wilderness—in these confusing, in-between times—Lester communicates what we need is direction, guidance, honesty, and solidarity. Those in the wilderness know they can't ever go back to where they came from, but they also aren't sure where God is leading them next. Hence, the importance of the wilderness.

As a nation, we are in such a wilderness. We have experienced a series of seismic shifts that have forever changed the faith landscape of our country, and we are now navigating confusion, disruption, and even distress. What are the seismic shifts that moved us into a wilderness season?

Rich Villodas, pastor of the wonderful New Life Church in Queens, New York, uses a helpful acronym to summarize these shifts. He says our nation needs CPR due to three forces: (1) Covid has had an immeasurable impact on every facet of our lived reality and continues to reshape the way we think about everything. (2) Political divisiveness and stridency are at an all-time high, and as a result, unity among God's people has been undercut and diminished in ways that often feel unprecedented. (3) Racial hostility continues to morph, evolve, and intensify. The racial landscape changed dramatically after the death of George Floyd (as well as other precious lives), and though there was a brief period of heightened conversation, we are now in the midst of a White backlash that has turned critical race theory into a boogeyman and targeted curricula that teach racial history.

Taken together, these three forces have forever changed the world as we know it. As Lester communicates in *All God's Children*, we must move forward and confront the old ways things have been done in order to learn a new way of standing in solidarity with one another. Essentially, we must move into a new way of relating and commit to this type of change. But as true as that is, it also raises difficult questions. What exactly needs to change? And what does that change look like? And how do we participate meaningfully and practically in seeking that change? These are wilderness questions. They are questions that come in the in-between times as we navigate confusion and disorientation.

It is exactly at this point where *All God's Children* becomes a balm for the soul and Terence emerges as just the guide that we need as we learn to navigate this confusing wilderness. One of the first stories you will read about Terence is his experience of pastoring in both a Black church and a White church amid the forces listed above. From this special vantage point, he is able to help us listen in on critical conversations and learn invaluable lessons for the journey ahead. The uniqueness of Terence's vantage point then continues to shine throughout his book. He is pastoring those of us reading it and creating a roadmap for how to move forward through this wilderness.

And for those of you who are White, as I am, this is especially important. If nothing else, this wilderness is a season of revealing and of reckoning. It is critical that we do not miss the opportunity to see what we do not see and learn what we do not currently understand. Nobody ever comes out of a wilderness the same. We are always formed in the wilderness, one way or the other. We become harder or softer, warmer or colder, more curious or more deeply dug in, more open or more distant, more gracious or angrier. As you prepare to read this book, I invite you to open your heart and view it as a handbook for navigating the wilderness our nation is in. Allow Terence to pastor you in your quest for deeper formation that leads toward greater sight, greater understanding, and ultimately greater love for God and neighbor.

EVERYONE HAS A STORY

I never thought I'd write a book on race. It was not in my plans at all.

One reason is that for a decade I have been focused intently on anti-poverty work challenging systems of White supremacy through advocating for those who are poor and marginalized in the United States. The nonprofit organization I started alongside my wife in 2013, Love Beyond Walls, advocates for the unhoused community, which means most of my days are spent in communication with people who have been overlooked by society, who live underneath bridges or out of their cars while trying to work a job or trying to find their sense of worth and belonging while living on the streets. This work has brought me before all of God's children, including people who are Brown, Black, White, Asian, Indigenous, Latinx, and a whole spectrum of people from various backgrounds. As I have always said, relating to the heartbeat of when Martin Luther King Jr. decided to stand against poverty in Memphis, poverty affects everyone; it does not discriminate.

It was only in recent years that I felt compelled to link the work of antiracism to my anti-poverty work in how I explain their intersectionality explicitly. When I think back to the summer of 2020, it was as if the "triple evils" MLK Jr. warned about converged on us all at once. We saw in plain sight the effects of poverty, racism, and militarism front and center. As our nation faced a global pandemic, I tackled the poverty issue by offering access to sanitation for those experiencing homelessness. It was my goal to keep them protected against a virus no one knew anything about. Then the murders of Ahmaud Arbery, George Floyd, and Breonna Taylor forced many to confront the racial trauma, injustice, and division in our country in a deeper way. As these protests escalated, pictures of police in military garb filled the TV screen.

As these scenes continued to unfold, I realized I had a voice to lend to the conversation. In fact, I needed to lend my voice to the conversation challenging systems of White supremacy. As a Black man with Black children who is mostly serving in communities that are Black and Brown, I noticed those in these communities looked for words from me; especially those who wrestled with poverty wanted to know why racism and oppression always seem to go hand in hand. And while I do acknowledge that race and class should not be conflated because they have their distinctions, it is important to see the interconnection and intersectionality between the two and how one upholds the other. I think this is why Reverend William Barber II expanded on MLK's triple evils to include ecological devastation and a call for national morality. Rev. Barber made it clear that bad policies, grounded in White supremacy, create a violent culture toward the poor and BIPOC (Black, Indigenous, and people of color) communities.[1] There is a strong difference between race and class, but it's important to note there are many overlapping factors at play. As

Patricia Hill Collins notes, "Social science research in the United States generally views social class less as a cause of other social phenomena, such as family structures and dynamics, and more as an outcome of such phenomena."[2] In other words, many of the class issues we face today exist because of systemic racial injustice.

While I have always known race impacts class in a profound way, I realized in 2020 I needed to do and say more about their connection. I suppose what really made me speak up was my growing fatigue at seeing racial injustice impact those I advocate for every day—which are people of color experiencing homelessness and poverty who are overrepresented.[3] I also grew tired of the constant battle I face as a Black man and the subtle ways racism affects me day to day. The conversation became personal for me. Jemar Tisby says, "All racial justice is relational," and I think he is right. As Tisby goes on to state:

> What sparks the desire for people to see change? How does someone develop a burden to combat racism? Often it comes through relationships with other people who are most adversely impacted by racist ideas and deeds. It is through knowing others that those we previously viewed as "problems" become people.[4]

I know this was the case for me. The more I took note of the stories of my own accounts with racism, and the stories of others in my life, the larger I realized the problem was, and the more I knew I had to lend my voice.

SEEING BEYOND THE SURFACE

Everyone has a story, a history that shapes who they are. Some stories are filled with happiness, while others are marked with seasons of intense pain. For the past decade, I have spent a great deal of time trying to learn the stories of others. Often these stories have come from people with social, economic, or cultural upbringings different from my own.

This work has been difficult because it requires decentering oneself and an enormous amount of compassion and empathy to show up and be fully present with others while walking with them through the darkest moments of their lives. So often when we see others who don't look, act, or talk like us or who are not part of our social circle, our gut reaction is to look aside or even walk the other way. The bigger the difference, the stronger the impulse. However, the irony is that we all want to be seen and noticed in some way. We want to be seen and acknowledged in our families, at our jobs, in our communities, in our relationships with our close friends, and among people whom we have never met.

Being seen is about having our humanity affirmed. Essentially, we all want to be seen as persons who possess worth, dignity, and humanity. Because we are all God's children, we want people to see us. Yet as much as we desire that, we often forget and even refuse to see others simply because we view them as different from ourselves.[5] So we refuse to acknowledge they exist, as though they were a bad movie playing on the fringes of our life that we would rather turn off than engage with.

Inattentional blindness is the refusal to acknowledge the existence of what's around you. It suggests you can be around something or someone and not give it or that person any attention. I would push this theory a little further to say the same thing could be true when it comes to acknowledging the history shaping other people, especially those who are unlike us. The term *inattentional blindness* was coined by two psychologists, Arien Mack and Irvin Rock, who published a book by the same name. They performed several experiments to understand how one could be proximate to something without paying full attention to it, thus rendering oneself blind to it.

Many scholars have expanded on their ideas, but the foundation of their thesis is that if we are consciously unaware of what is around us, we could miss it or the person in our proximity, causing problems structurally and racially.

According to the American Psychological Association, Mack and Rock's research explains this phenomenon:

In Mack and Rock's standard procedure, they presented a small cross briefly on a computer screen and asked participants to judge which arm of the cross was longer. After several trials, an unexpected object, such as a brightly colored rectangle, appeared on the screen along with the cross. Mack and Rock report that participants busy paying attention to the cross often failed to notice the unexpected object even when it had appeared in the center of their field of vision. When participants' attention was not diverted by the cross, they easily noticed such objects. Following these initial findings, Mack and Rock discovered that participants were more likely to notice their own names or a happy face than stimuli that were not as meaningful to them, such as another name or an upside-down face. Finally, the team found that even though participants did not detect the presence of unattended words that were presented on a computer screen, such stimuli nonetheless exerted an implicit influence on participants' later performance on a word-completion task. Mack says, "I came away from our studies convinced that there's no conscious perception without attention." She adds that the findings also led her to suspect that the brain undertakes considerable perceptual processing outside of conscious awareness before attention is engaged and that objects or events that are personally meaningful are most likely to capture people's attention.[6]

While exploring this disconnect between the unhoused community and those who are unwilling to acknowledge them and their stories, I constantly found parallels in what those experiencing homelessness face and my own experience with being a Black man in America. As a Black man, there are times, almost weekly, when I have to deal with people who do not want to see me or know my story simply because they prejudge me based on the color of my skin. To be Black in this country is to be reminded of our blackness every single time we encounter discrimination.

In 1961, James Baldwin, a well-known writer and thinker who still contributes to the shaping of Black intellect, was asked by a radio host what it was like to be Black in America, and he said:

> To be a Negro in this country and to be relatively conscious is to be in a state of rage almost, almost all of the time— and in one's work. And part of the rage is this: It isn't only what is happening to you. But it's what's happening all around you and all of the time in the face of the most extraordinary and criminal indifference, indifference of most white people in this country, and their ignorance.[7]

I have felt deeply hurt each time I have encountered a White person who has ignored me rather than engaged with me simply because I was Black. Each time it reminds me of the historical suffering of my community and how much my ancestors gave just for me to be seen as God's child, deserving of love, equality, equity, fairness, and justice. Imagine walking down the street and having a group of White professionals cross the street because they see a six-foot-two Black man walking toward them. Or being in an elevator where White women clutch their purses and White men step back to avoid standing beside you. Imagine standing in line at a store next to White people who are waiting to be served and, although you had arrived first, being greeted last; it's essentially what Mack and Rock discovered: "There's no conscious perception without attention."

Alongside my work with those experiencing homelessness, it has become my mission to ensure that no one feels invisible. As a Black person, I know what it's like to see Black people silenced when trying to communicate our worth or views. I know the feeling of being overlooked and unheard when I have needed to share stories that have threatened my blackness, indeed my very existence, to majority culture. What if we learned to look past our biases and challenge our embedded ideologies that tell us to treat people differently when they come from a different social location? What if instead we adopted the approach of immersing ourselves in other people's stories to experience empathy and connection?

THE SUBTLETY OF RACISM

As the leader of Love Beyond Walls, I'm given the opportunity to walk in many different spaces, including Black, Brown, and White communities. Many of these circles are wonderful, but there have been numerous points where I have faced some form of discrimination.

For example, during the Covid-19 pandemic, I was invited by one of my White friends to meet a group of all-White real estate developers to talk about creating more safe spaces in city landscapes that do not discriminate against people who are unhoused. The meeting was after work, and given the fact that most of my daily interactions are with those who are unhoused and battling poverty in our community, my attire of choice that day was a hoodie and jeans. On top of this, one of my social distancing practices during Covid-19 included not visiting a barber, so my hair had grown out. Needless to say, I stood out in stark contrast to the White businessmen in pristine business suits.

As I walked in, I felt the eyes of everyone in the room focus on me. Some looked at my hair, others at my dress, and others at my frame. It is the type of feeling you get when you are stared at with suspicion, instead of welcomed into a place. When I sat down I knew something was off because I could sense the tension in the room with these guys who barely knew me. My palms started to sweat. I had been in dozens of similar meetings, and so I knew it wasn't lack of confidence. It was fear of being judged, of being Black, of being different from them.

My friend tried to put the room at ease and said, "Hey, Terence, why don't you tell everyone about your work?" And so I started to share. As I did, I made my best attempt at sharing in such a way that put everyone at ease. I answered some of the internal questions I knew were circling in their minds: *Why is this guy here in a hoodie and jeans? How many Black nonprofit leaders lead thriving organizations? Does this guy know what he's doing?* I felt this need to validate myself.

And as I shared, it wasn't long before the trickle of condescending questions began. "Terence, where did you get your education?" "How large a budget have you operated?" "Is Love Beyond Walls a valid organization?" "Is it an actual 501c3?"

Finally, my friend jumped to my defense. "Hey, guys, Terence knows what he's talking about. He's an expert and has lectured in many places."

But by that point, the damage had already been done. And it's been hundreds of similar encounters that have convinced me of the fact that racism is still alive and well in America today, and we must do something about it before it creates more harm to BIPOC people and communities. This is a reality we all must face. As David Gillborn writes, "If we are to change the racial (and racist) status quo, we must refuse the growing mainstream assertion that racism is irrelevant or even non-existent."[8] Instead, we must remove the blinders from our eyes and take full notice of the lives impacted by systemic racial injustice. We must see people as God sees them.

Some mentalities influenced by racism and White supremacy often reveal themselves subtly in ways that may not seem harmful but are actually quite harmful. Resisting these types of mindsets requires the power of story. Story and reframing are at the core of solidarity work. Knowing a person's story and even perhaps the collective history of their community could be the first step in also acknowledging someone's dignity and humanity. But it's not just about knowing and acknowledging someone's story—we must give that person or persons space to own their own narrative without tampering with their story. Such was the case with my friend Leonard.

MEETING LEONARD

I met Leonard one day as I was filling up my car at a service station. He stumbled up to a nearby waste bin and began rummaging through its contents. He looked to be in his sixties and wore overalls, a short-sleeved shirt, and a pair of shoes with holes big enough for his sockless feet to stick out the front. He tried to be quiet as he searched the trashcan for a meal. He kept his head down and did not make eye contact with me or anyone else. I knew that look. It's one born from the kind of shame that settles in after you've been repeatedly made to feel insignificant.

I called out to him and asked if he would come over. He looked up, and I noticed a slight spark in his eyes, clearly surprised someone had noticed him. When he made his way over on shaky legs, I asked him his name and how his day was going. Addressing someone by their name may not seem like a lot, but to those who have been made to feel invisible, it is deeply affirming. And while it might sound unusual to ask someone looking for lunch in a trashcan how their day is going, I often do so intentionally. This particular question offers people dignity, confirms that they have been seen and acknowledged, and, if they wish, offers them the space to share in full honesty where they are and how they got there.

While most people who have been shunned by society remain guarded in their response, Leonard was not, and he went on to share his entire story. He had lost his wife and then, due to depression, everything else: his job, home, family, friends, absolutely everything. He said he was trying not to bother anyone at the gas station and would be on his way as soon as he found something to eat. I assured him he wasn't bothering me or anyone else, and as my truck filled up with gas, our conversation deepened until I found the courage to ask him a more personal question.

"Leonard, if you had one wish, what would it be?"

Without hesitation, he responded, "I wish I could be made over."

For a moment, I thought he meant that he wanted to start his life over and perhaps make different choices. But as he plucked at his soiled shirt and ragged beard, the debris and dirt falling from both like snow, I realized he meant something different entirely. He simply wished for a wash and maybe a trim. A makeover!

All Leonard wanted was a shower and the feeling of dignity that comes from being clean. I knew there were shelters that offered services like this, but there were usually strings attached, making the reward not worth the risk. Besides, the closest shelter was more than ten miles away. That would have been a long hike even for me, at half this man's age and with a full belly.

This exchange reminded me of how critical it is to make connections with people that go beyond the surface. As many people do every day, I could have looked at Leonard through a lens of disdain and used my imagination to think of everything that might have caused him to end up on the street. But it was more important to take the time to hear his unique story.

Ironically, there are many similarities between how those who are experiencing homelessness are treated and those who are Black are treated. When you live without an address, people look through you, fear you, call the police on you, discriminate against you, and even spew harsh and damaging words at you. The same could be said for those of us who live in Black skin. People of color are systematically overlooked, feared because of an unfair mischaracterization, discriminated against in public spaces and in organizations, and subject to dehumanizing and unwarranted narratives. Consider table 1 and its parallel nature.

Table 1. My experiences

Experiences While Experiencing Homelessness	Experiences as a Black Person
Criminalized for existing in public spaces	Criminalized for existing in public spaces
Overlooked and mistreated for experiencing homelessness	Overlooked and mistreated for being Black
Socially excluded for being unhoused	Socially excluded for being Black
Feared for experiencing homelessness	Feared for being Black
Discriminated against for experiencing homelessness	Discriminated against for skin color
Constantly fighting false narratives for experiencing homelessness	Constantly fighting false narratives and anti-blackness

In a real sense, I had a deep empathy for Leonard because I felt his pain, albeit in a different way. Because of this, I couldn't help but see him as a beloved child of God. It's only when we allow people into our lives to share their individual and collective stories that we begin to recognize their humanity alongside our own, and, in turn, we can extend empathy, compassion, and understanding to them. I believe this is what MLK Jr. was getting at when he described his picture for the beloved community. King cast a clear vision immediately following the bus boycott in Montgomery, Alabama. Once he heard about the Supreme Court victory, he stated:

> The end [of the Civil Rights Movement] is reconciliation; the end is redemption; the end is the creation of the Beloved Community. It is this type of spirit and this type of love that can transform opposers into friends. It is this type of understanding goodwill that will transform the deep gloom of the old age into the exuberant gladness of the new age. It is this love which will bring about miracles in the hearts of men.[9]

King's beloved community was a vision that all members of society, regardless of social location, would have access to all that society has to offer.

In the end, my conversation with Leonard proved fruitful. Love Beyond Walls helped him get off the streets and connected him with senior housing and access to the necessities all people deserve. But something bigger happened because of our chance meeting. Leonard's story inspired one of the most pivotal campaigns we have ever had at Love Beyond Walls, the Mobile Makeover Unit.

Thanks to Leonard, it dawned on me how we could use the bus—a thirty-passenger model gifted to us by a Madison, Georgia, church for a one-dollar donation—to serve Atlanta's unhoused community. In addition to providing transportation to those in need, we would convert the thirty-seat vehicle into a mobile hygiene station, complete with a shower and a clothes closet. For the first time, we would be able to provide a feeling of humanity to anyone anywhere in the city. Motivated by

Leonard's story, we would offer thousands the opportunity to step out of the shadows and be seen.

Looking back, it was only when I allowed myself to hear Leonard's story that my heart gained more compassion to stand in solidarity with those who are without an address. I did not determine what I thought he needed, but I discovered how he truly felt. As a result, I was able to see the bigger picture for the entire community.

HISTORY IMPACTS STORY

The Mobile Makeover Unit was radical and unlike anything the city had seen. Like most opportunities to create great change, it faced equally great resistance. I had to figure out a way to inspire support for this makeover project, especially when so many people believe that projects like it are merely a waste of time and resources for people like Leonard.

In an effort to educate people, cultivate empathy, and make this bus what we envisioned it to be, I came up with a "Get on the Bus" campaign. To bring awareness to the lack of access to sanitation for those experiencing homelessness, I pledged to live on top of the bus for one month. It was my hope that in doing so, we could draw attention to those who, like Leonard, needed clean clothes and safe places to shower.

Dave, a friend who had a background in carpentry, agreed to build a stable platform on top of the bus where I could stay in a tent for thirty days and thirty nights. With my wife's and children's blessings, I prepared to do this in the middle of winter. In December 2014, I shared my plan on social media and, as expected, drew both criticism and praise. I actually received a few anonymous death threat emails, and someone even created a spam account posing as me and bashing me and my family, calling me a "cult leader."

Then I received one of the most disturbing emails I've ever had during my time as executive director of Love Beyond Walls. In no uncertain terms, it claimed that I was a horrible father and husband and that I was insane for bringing attention to bums on the street during Christmas. "Who leaves their family for bums?" the email ranted, informing me that it would be cold and that I could die. It ended with, "How could you do this? You should reconsider."

Although I knew I would face opposition, I had not expected such a personal attack. As I sat staring in silence at my computer screen, a thought crossed my mind more than once: *There's no way anyone could say these things if they knew Leonard's story. Surely if they heard what Leonard told me, they'd be just as compelled as I am to do whatever was needed.*

In the days leading up to the launch of this campaign, I reflected on how detrimental it is when people fear those with different cultural upbringings and experiences from their own. That fear and hatred diminish the confidence and self-worth of those who it's directed toward. I remember my friend Tyrus telling me how it damaged his self-worth when people threw cans at him, locked their doors on him, and hurled expletives at him because he was unhoused. He told me, "People don't even know me, my story, or how I arrived at homelessness, yet they fear me. I am a father, cousin, son, brother, and a friend. I am Tyrus. I am somebody."

When we unfairly criticize people we have never met and assign stories to them that may be untrue, it dishonors not only the ones being criticized but God as well. Every BIPOC person—Black, Asian, Latinx, Middle Eastern, North African, Pacific Islander, or Indigenous—embodies the image of their Creator. All people deserve to have their inherent dignity recognized and affirmed. When we choose to dishonor the image of God in people, we are communicating to God that this part of his creation is inferior.

Conversely, when we choose to immerse ourselves in people's stories and history, the way we view them cannot help but change. We must endeavor to become proximate to their history. The author of the hurtful email had not taken the time to hear these accounts and therefore could not understand my actions. The missing connection became clear. President Barack Obama said it best in remarks he gave at a student roundtable: "Learning to stand in somebody else's shoes to see through their eyes, that's how peace begins. And it's up to you to make that happen."[10]

There was more to that cruel email than merely a failure to understand the people I served. The words were a personal attack. In addition to not knowing the stories of the people I hoped to help, he did not know my story. Because he didn't know my story, he had no perspective from which to understand me. He carried a set of beliefs about me and my motives based on his life and experiences. A broader application and realization began to materialize as I thought about this interaction. This need to know people's histories to empathize with them was not limited to those seeking food and shelter. In our present moment, more than ever, people are in close proximity, yet we don't really know each other.

THE IMPORTANCE OF BLACK HISTORY

You cannot understand people's stories without understanding their history. You cannot understand Black people in the present moment without understanding how history has affected them. Ignoring that history can lead to all sorts of misconceptions. I learned this lesson once again back in 2015–2018.

During that season, I held two simultaneous pastorships: one at a predominantly White church, the other at a historically Black church, both in the heart of Atlanta. Never in my wildest dreams did I think I'd be pastoring these two very different spaces as a Black man. Both churches acknowledged Jesus, but they had very different ways of relating the hope of Jesus to their realities. Honestly, existing in two separate spaces where both my role and my experiences were understood, regarded, and treated differently is one of the hardest things I've ever done. At times it was one of the most hurtful experiences I have undergone in Christian ministry.

Amid the intense racial tension pervading our country, I found myself feeling misunderstood and silenced in the predominately White space because there was often no mention of the terror that was affecting me and the Black community I showed up in as a pastor as well. Each setting had very different ways of sharing the gospel, loving the community, and standing with those affected by racial suffering. I already experienced trauma every time racial tension and violence against Black people was reported in the news. Sometimes the silence from the White church or its dismissal of Black people's actions when they began to protest and cry out from the hurt and rage they were feeling collectively only added to the trauma. Racial trauma was not supposed to be a part of my journey in the faith, but it was. Sheila Wise Rowe defines racial trauma as "the physical and psychological symptoms that people of color often experience after a stressful racist incident."[11]

When I was in the White church space, I found myself caught between two worlds where the breakdown of communication between brothers and sisters based on cultural dynamics and long-held perceptions of the world and each other kept empathy and understanding at bay. Whenever I found myself in this predominantly White space, I felt the need to share the missing narratives and historical context behind the Black struggle that went far beyond the issue of slavery. Sometimes, I was afforded the opportunity to speak freely in small ways among a few people at a time. I did notice that some of my White congregants began to set aside their prejudices and fears, but most maintained their distance and worldviews that sometimes clashed with my realities as a Black man.

In contrast, on Sundays in church with the Black congregation, talking about social issues from the pulpit and preaching messages of liberation against racial violence were a part of the liturgy. There was no separation between being Black and being Christian. I didn't feel like I had to edit and censor my blackness based on how it would be perceived as I attempted to connect my current realities with my collective history as a Black person. I could love God and lament as a Black man at the same time because God was big enough to handle them both. The times when I was given the opportunity to talk about this in a predominately White space were always accompanied by long emails about how it was Marxist, liberal, or me being influenced by CNN, and never about how this might just be my reality as a Black man living in this country.

As I continued to relay the history of the Black struggle to those unaware of its context and relevance today, I realized that, as Black people, we carry the weight of our generational history deep within us. As I shared with the predominately White congregation the unfulfilled promises and the failed social contract with the Black community throughout America's history, I noticed that a few of the people sincerely wanted to learn or held genuine empathy toward their Black brothers and sisters and the historical struggle they continue to bear. As I humanized Leonard's story, I found that humanizing my own struggle in the Black experience generated greater empathy while also dismantling stereotypes and prejudices to those who were willing to listen and lean in.

During your journey through this book, my hope is that it encourages you to learn about and understand other people's stories and histories on a deeper level. In doing so, I pray it helps you dismantle unrecognized prejudice, encourage understanding, cultivate advocacy and friendship, and become a person who is ready to create a world that centers racial healing and solidarity and lifts Black and Brown voices.

As you explore the topic of race, especially if you are White, I challenge you not to judge others based on secondhand information or long-held presumptions. Instead, honor people by getting to know their full stories in a way that offers a sense of solidarity and connectedness without the filter of censorship. While this concept is important on a basic level, it should also serve as a building block and be applied more broadly. I understand that there are many books on the topic of race, ranging from historical to current events. However, I would like to approach this topic through my personal experiences to give context to how some persons might relate to my story as they navigate spaces that are toxic and in which racism is swept under the rug of inaction. If I am honest, some of my words will pierce deeply because they come from a place of deep reflection. This is a topic people of every ethnicity and culture need to understand because we all need to grow in understanding, empathy, and solidarity with others who emerge from different social locations.

I also discuss some historical and current events along the way to express the urgency for people to know others more deeply and become peacemakers and antiracists in resistance against White supremacy. I'll explore some hidden history of Black people, as well as the ways I've struggled to understand my own history, and how learning that history has given me greater compassion and the ability to build relationships cross-culturally. In the process, I hope my story will inspire you to look at race relations through a new lens and recognize we are all God's children. As Dr. Christina Edmonson writes, "Being a faithful antiracist is an art, not a formulaic process. Like painting a picture, building a chair, shaping a dress, or crafting a meal, it requires knowledge, skill, experience, and creativity."[12]

By the end of this book, I hope to have provided a bridge that people from different ways of life can cross, shedding their prejudices and fears with every step. It is only after having crossed safely to the other side of that bridge that empathy and long-term healing and solidarity can begin, at long last, to exist.

A PAST I COULD NOT TOUCH

Dad, why are there tanks on the TV? And why did that man have his knee on the neck of that other man?" These words came from the lips of my nine-year-old son, a little more than a month into the US Covid-19 pandemic. As the world sat at home in isolation, many watched in horror as news outlets replayed the death of George Floyd. Eight minutes and forty-six seconds was all it took for his life to be snuffed out, his body lying motionless on a Minneapolis street. Pictures of Floyd's lifeless Black body circulated around digital media, causing many to speak out against racial injustice and the violence against Black people. The public's reaction was strong.

Crowds of protesters in Atlanta and around the country and world poured into the streets to mourn this loss and to stand against oppression. Companies and sports leagues that had remained silent on this topic for years sprang into action. Civic leaders demanded change.

For others, this nationwide response generated fear, causing some politicians to take aggressive action. Tanks, SWAT teams, and police officers in body armor were called in to "keep the peace."

As my wife, Cecilia, and I watched in shock and silence as the events unfolded on our basement TV, Terence II, or TJ as we like to call him, poked his head around the corner to see what was going on. Usually, whenever this happened, his curiosity would subside the moment he saw whatever "boring events" his mom and dad found interesting. We were still in quarantine because of strict Covid-19 protocols, and our children were at home with us most days.

This day was different. The images on the screen gripped his attention, and his tender heart could make little sense of what he saw. He heard the audio of Floyd calling out for his mother just seconds before his death, and it left him with all sorts of questions—questions I felt no parent should ever have to answer. I'm sure it resonated with his nine-year-old brain because he had called out for his mom numerous times as a child.

What happened next was a scene that played out in many Black households that day. I sat my son down to give him "the Talk." Not the "birds and bees" one, but the conversation most Black parents have with their children, the Talk that is foreign to White households in America, when Black parents painstakingly explain that the innocent world in which our children are raised is not all it seems.

In fact, the Talk I gave him later became a TEDx talk[1] on how to talk to Black children in a world of racial injustice. As Black adults, we know that the Talk warns Black children that there are people out there who dislike them simply because of the color of their skin. It was the Talk my mom gave me and that her parents gave her.

This conversation included the following nuggets of wisdom:

- "Never walk alone in a store."
- "Always keep your hands out of your pockets when you walk into a store."
- "If you don't have money, do not even go into a store."
- "If people are watching you while you are shopping, pull your money out of your pocket and make it visible."
- "When you drive and get pulled over, keep your hands on the wheel."
- "Do not wear baggy clothes, and keep your hair cut short."
- "Because you are a young Black man, you already have two strikes against you."
- "Never pick up anything if you don't intend to buy it."
- "Never look angry or sad in public because you could be viewed as a threat."

The first time I heard my mom share some of these examples, it seemed like I was drinking out of a firehose. There was so much to process, and it felt like my secure little world had been shattered. When I raised my two children, I took a slightly different approach, although the reality is that I know my wife and I can only do so much to prepare them for a world that might mistreat them because they are Black. Even before they could speak,[2] I would pull TJ and his sister, Zion, into my bedroom every morning and affirm their identity. I made sure they knew their worth, their value, how much potential they had, and the long legacy of our Black heritage. I told them they were leaders while also validating their joy and bolstering their confidence. I did this because I knew what it was like to grow up as a Black child and have racism thrown in my face long before I knew it had a name through the images I saw on television. I saw how Black people were treated when encountering whiteness.

I talked to my children with a deep sense of joy as well as sorrow and humiliation, grieving that any parent should have these conversations with their little ones. But it was this foundation that paved the way for the conversation I had with my son that afternoon, one in which I shared with TJ many of the guidelines my mom had shared with me. We talked about what it means to be a Black man in our culture today and about some of the special challenges he would face as he grew up in a racist society. Honestly, it is one of the hardest conversations I have ever had with my son.

After our conversation, my son asked if we could do our own form of peaceful protest at home for George Floyd. Together, we got some markers and pieces of cardboard, and I asked him what he wanted to write. Recalling Floyd's dying words to his mother, TJ took out a marker and wrote, "I am a Black son." Following his lead, I wrote my own sign, "I am a Black dad." I cried a lot after this experience because I knew that regardless of how my son and I showed up to protest, it would not erase the past, bring back George Floyd, or take away the disdain and racial bias that some people have against Black people. However, I did it with pride because I was teaching my son that his worth has nothing to do with how we are treated collectively by whiteness. It was a conversation that I refused to hide or bury.

Our talk was a stark reminder for me that White supremacy and the racism of previous generations continue to leave their mark today, and those who seek to ignore it preserve a part of history that comes out through the unchecked beliefs and behaviors of people who harbor this type of hatred. Anderson, Caughy, and Owen write:

> "The Talk" refers to a specific type of racial socialization message that many Black parents have with their children about how to safely conduct themselves when interacting

with police officers and other individuals in positions of power. With the recent increased exposure of racialized violence against Black people at the hands of police and vigilantes in the United States, many parents of young Black children now feel especially compelled to initiate these conversations to equip their children with the necessary knowledge to protect themselves when interacting with police officers. Black parents bear the unjust burden of striking a balance between alerting their children of possible harm while also not villainizing every member of law enforcement their child may encounter.[3]

A HISTORY I WAS NEVER TAUGHT

I was given the same talk I gave my son, but I did not learn about the depths of Black history until I was out of high school, and I wanted to ensure that my son didn't have that experience. Imagine growing up and going through your K–12 experience only covering topics that spoke casually to your identity as a Black child, and then once you get out of high school being immersed in a world where the opportunities to learn about your background, heritage, and history are slim to none. You may experience mistreatment due to being Black, but understanding the depths of the structural and systemic history and its implications is a challenge when you are not given a chance to learn these things in school. A recent example of this is when Texas education officials proposed to rename "slavery" to "involuntary relocation," which was eventually struck down for attempting to downplay the effects of enslavement.[4]

Over time I have learned how intentional this was from my education, and many others'. LaGarrett King, a distinguished professor, traces the depiction and intentional removal of Black history from history books in the K–12 experience. He examines literature from 1890 to 1940, the long history of how

Black people were depicted in schoolbooks, and how it was all driven by whiteness and dominated by White males. He writes,

> K–12 social studies textbooks [were] written by White historians and educators who used history as a means to explore ideas of U.S. citizenship. It was common in these textbooks to underscore Black persons as inferior and second-class citizens. Early social studies textbooks emphasized that the "Black skin was a curse" (Woodson, 1933 p. 3) through narratives that purported that Black people were naturally "barbarians," "destitute of intelligence," or "having little humanity" (Brown, 2010; Elson, 1964; Foster, 1999).

He goes on to say that the racialization of blackness was used as a justification for the paternalistic attitudes White citizens had toward Black people.[5] The erasure of history from schoolbooks took place as a way of keeping Black history away from Black people who might have an opportunity to truly know themselves.

Those in power have often downplayed the role of the enslavement of Africans in the formation of this country's economy to silence those who see and feel the link between enslavement and today's racial struggles. MLK notes:

> For many African-American educators, early conceptions of social studies educations did not achieve this and [were] disconnected from the political, cultural, or economic realities of the race. For example, numerous White educators believed that Western epistemologies, through the social studies, would help serve as the conduits for the cultural and intellectual development of African Americans.[6]

Slavery has been described as a peculiar institution, a regional issue relegated to pockets of the antebellum South and limited in its national economic effects. But this description is false. In Edward E. Baptist's historical masterpiece, *The Half Has Never Been Told: Slavery and the Making of American Capitalism*, we learn through well-documented accounts of that time that America's economic supremacy was built almost entirely on the backs of those who were enslaved. Summarizing the reasons behind the apparent contradiction, Baptist offers the following explanation:

> All these assumptions lead to still more implications, ones that shape attitudes, identities, and debates about policy. If slavery was outside of US history, for instance— if indeed it was a drag and not a rocket booster to American economic growth—then slavery was not implicated in US growth, success, power, and wealth. Therefore, none of the massive quantities of wealth and treasure piled by that economic growth is owed to African Americans. Ideas about slavery's history determine the ways in which Americans hope to resolve the long contradiction between the claims of the United States to be a nation of freedom and opportunity, on the one hand, and, on the other, the unfreedom, the unequal treatment, and the opportunity denied that for most of American history have been the reality faced by people of African descent.[7]

The degree to which slavery contributed to the superiority of the US economy is only one of many areas in which history has been skewed, forgotten, or replaced with fiction. *Lies My Teacher Told Me: Everything Your American History Textbook Got Wrong*, by James W. Loewen, explores further harmful discrepancies, many of them less about ignoring the harm done and more about forgetting the major roles people of color played in bringing about the modern society we enjoy today.

Loewen shows how reading modern textbooks would lead anyone to believe that only the White people of the Western world, for instance, should be credited with our understanding of world geography and the peoples that exist within it. But a careful study of those peoples paints a different picture. Loewen writes:

> So long as our textbooks hide from us the roles that people of color have played in exploration, from at least 6000 BC to the twentieth century, they encourage us to look to Europe and its extensions as the seat of all knowledge and intelligence. So long as they say "discover," they imply that whites are the only people who really matter. So long as they simply celebrate Columbus, rather than teach both sides of his exploit, they encourage us to identify with White Western exploitation rather than study it.[8]

There was a time when all this information was news to me. Yes, I understood as a teenager that there were bleak points in America's history. But from the textbooks we read throughout my K–12 experience, those were just moments in time, limited to certain areas of the Deep South. The enslavement of Africans and Black oppression was despicable, but I was educated to believe that we had moved past that time. In fact, I recall one White US History teacher in high school telling me in front of an all-Black classroom that *the mistakes of the past had no weight for Black people today.*

However, a conversation with my grandfather changed all that.

MY GRANDFATHER'S WORDS

When I was seventeen, I bought a 1981 Chevrolet Caprice from one of my best friends and his dad, who was a father figure to me. My friend's name is Atif Shaw, and his dad, Artie, was a positive role model in my teenage years. Back then, the only thing I put more effort into than getting into trouble was saving up to buy that car. It was beautiful, with a baby blue and white top exterior and a navy blue interior. Like any used car, it had issues: the right window wouldn't roll down, sometimes the air conditioner wouldn't work, and there was no heat in the winter. I had to wait for the warmth of the motor to make its way through the vents just to defrost the windows. But I loved that car. It looked great, and it got me around most of the time—until it didn't.

Have you ever had that experience where you go to press the brake pedal but the car doesn't slow down? That was me one hot afternoon in July. I was coming back from playing basketball at the park and preparing to come to a stop, but my car had other intentions. With all the power I could muster, I pressed down hard on the brake pedal, finally grinding it to a halt. The brake booster had gone out.

I had only owned the car for seven months, and I was already having problems. Not a good sign. Soon I began contacting mechanics in my area. But each quote I received left me more discouraged. There was no way I could afford what they would charge me.

Overhearing my conversations, Mom told me to call my grandfather.

Carlton York was a mechanic by trade and had every tool in his garage to prove it. Air compressors, socket sets, and car jacks were just a few of his many tools that I knew nothing about. I had never touched a socket wrench before in my life and had no intention of breaking this pattern in the foreseeable future. But Granddaddy had other plans. After I gave him a call about the car, he told me to drive it over, and he would show me how to fix it. I didn't like the sound of that.

Easing the shiny Caprice into his driveway, I noticed he was primed and ready to go. There was no chitchat and no "great to see you, Terence." Instead, like a character out of a movie, my granddad strapped a flashlight on his head and slid under the car, motioning for me to do the same. It was as if he had been waiting for this moment my entire life.

Before I finished shimmying into position, my granddad handed me a socket and began motioning toward different parts above me.

"Okay, so first, you loosen that bolt, then that one, and don't forget that one over there. Then you pop this thing out. But be careful you don't bang your head in the process."

I cursed inside. This was not the sort of hands-on lesson I had in mind when I said I needed help.

Mustering what little willpower I had, I set to work. My progress was slow, and I realized that unscrewing a tight bolt in an awkward position was no simple task. After dropping the socket for the fifth time, my silent frustration boiled over.

"I can't do it," I muttered, not expecting the reaction those four words would generate.

Granddaddy's jaw tightened, and from his dark expression you would have thought I had spat in his face and called him a liar.

"Terence, I don't ever want to hear that word come out of your mouth again. Where we come from, 'can' is how you survive."

I paused, unsure how to respond and unaware of how those next few hours would change my life. As we lay under the front of my car with our backs caked in dirt, I had one of the deepest conversations I had ever had with my grandfather.

He told me about growing up during a segregated era, how he went to an all-Black high school, drank out of "colored" water fountains, how if he had driven this car when he was my age, the police would have stopped him every time he came or went. "Hell, they stopped me on my bike just to remind me they were in charge," he told me. He reminded me it wasn't that long ago that the police were formed in this country for the specific purpose of capturing escaped slaves. The NAACP has well-documented history of slave patrolling in America, which even includes a slave patrol oath in North Carolina.

The origins of modern-day policing can be traced back to the slave patrol. The earliest formal slave patrol was created in the Carolinas in the early 1700s with one mission: to establish a system of terror and squash slave uprisings with the capacity to pursue, apprehend, and return runaway slaves to their owners. Tactics included the use of excessive force to control and produce desired slave behavior. Patrollers signed an oath that read:

> I [patroller's name], do swear, that I will as searcher for guns, swords, and other weapons among the slaves in my district, faithfully, and as privately as I can, discharge the trust reposed in me as the law directs, to the best of my power. So help me, God.

Slave patrols continued until the end of the Civil War and the passage of the Thirteenth Amendment. Following the Civil War, during Reconstruction, slave patrols were replaced by militia-style groups who were empowered to control and deny freed slaves access to equal rights. They relentlessly and systematically enforced Black Codes, strict local and state laws that regulated and restricted access to labor, wages, voting rights, and general freedoms for formerly enslaved people.[9]

Granddaddy then told me about run-ins with the Ku Klux Klan. He described being chased for miles by a pickup truck before four men jumped out and beat him, forcing him to spend several days in a hospital. He told me stories about how he was almost lynched, and even writing this gives me chills.

Pausing this history lesson, he looked deep into my eyes and asked, "Have you been through anything like that?"

"No," I replied, too ashamed to say anything else.

"That's right," he said, "because we went through it for you. You can't have any fear, Terence. Now, take that socket and try again."

I did, and we finished the installation. By this point, my thoughts had shifted from the frustration of my broken-down car to the hardships Black people had experienced. Sure, I knew about some of these pains, but my knowledge had always come from a distance because of the lack of information in school. After this conversation, it was no longer buried. It was in my face and a part of me. Those brutal acts of racism I had heard occurred in the past and to people I did not know, but now they were part of my ancestry and thus part of my story.

Listening to my grandfather's experiences changed everything. For the first time in my life, I felt his pain, but I also understood our collective pain as Black people. Those distant, horrific stories were now personal because they happened to someone I talked to, touched, and interacted with. Someone I loved. He was—and is—my living history, and as I write this book, he is still alive.

My grandfather's words continue to echo in my mind to this very day. They came to mind in 2008 when the first Black man was elected president. "Yes, we can!" was more than a catchy campaign slogan for people like him who understood the long journey of oppression. For many Black people, including my grandfather, it symbolized the power of determination, resilience, and sacrifice. It symbolized moments of hope in the aftermath of collective pain. It was something that gave us hope of seeing the first biracial woman as vice president or the first

Black woman as a justice on the US Supreme Court—especially for women like my grandmother Gloria York, who would remind me of the mistreatment Black women experienced during enslavement and Jim Crow, and the mistreatment that still happens frequently in society today. It represented small changes from the past but also spoke to the history we must still unearth so those who are blinded to it can grapple with its realness and lingering effects.

MY JOURNEY INTO THE PAST

After hearing what my grandfather had lived through, I went on my own personal journey to better understand the history of my people. Because of the lack of information I'd received in school, I assumed there would be few books on this subject. But I couldn't have been more wrong. There were scores of titles detailing the historical struggles of Black people in society, and still more showing the link between that history and the persistent challenges of today, all written by Black people. I often wondered why these titles and authors were never spoken about in depth during school. Whether *Invisible Man* by Ralph Ellison, *Another Country* by James Baldwin, Zora Neale Hurston's *Mules and Men*, or *Song of Solomon* by Toni Morrison, each of these titles and more shaped my understanding of the struggle of Black people to gain equality.

In a recent book by Isabel Wilkerson, *Caste: The Origins of Our Discontents*, we're shown how society has always slotted Black people into a caste, one that is looked down on as well as deprived of critical advantages. She compares caste systems around the world to the American class system that was built on White supremacy. The book highlights the fact that while caste systems have been around for thousands of years and are not always based on race, in America, being Black immediately identifies one as a member of this lower strata.

In an interview with NPR, Wilkerson explains that

> caste focuses in on the infrastructure of our divisions and the rankings, whereas race is the metric that's used to determine one's place in that. Caste is the term that is more precise [than race]; it is more comprehensive, and it gets at the underlying infrastructure that often we cannot see, but that is there undergirding much of the inequality and injustices and disparities that we live with in this country.

This is history, but as Wilkerson painstakingly shows, it is also the Black condition here and now.

The more I looked around and developed my personal library of stories and history that centered my ancestors—both those who came before me (during enslavement) and those living in contemporary times who have recently passed away—the more I found. And the more I found, the more I understood why so much was being left out. Many years after my talk with Granddaddy, I was invited to preach in a fairly large, predominantly White church working intently on racial justice and healing. That my granddaddy agreed to come and listen was an accomplishment in itself. He'd never witnessed a Black person speaking to a largely White congregation, and, knowing he wouldn't be around forever, I asked if he wanted to come with my grandmother and hear me, and he agreed. After the service, he told me how scared he had felt the entire time. He was afraid that at any moment I might say something wrong, and that the congregation would turn on me. I could hear the trauma from White supremacy and racism coming through his words, and it broke my heart. Does it break yours?

When he was young, a situation like this would have caused him to fear for his life based on his encounters with the KKK.

This was hard for me to comprehend, but I could understand it somewhat, based on how racism still shows up today.

Imagine someone you care for and respect as a pillar of your life. Now picture that individual having to battle fear, not because they might have cancer or lose their job (things that most of us would agree are beyond our control), but because of real-life experiences and trauma stemming from the hands of other people filled with racial hatred.

What if it wasn't just your grandfather or grandmother, but also your parents and your aunts and uncles and your friends' parents and grandparents? What if the list went on and on until almost everyone you knew of a certain age had their own stories of how people of a particular segment of society had mistreated them? What if you saw it with your own eyes too? How would that make you feel?

I can tell you how I felt: angry, scared, confused, and upset that so much history had been buried. I realized my grandfather never got a chance to occupy White spaces without fear of something being done to him, let alone hearing his Black grandson preach to this audience as they listened. Many Black persons still fear harm in White spaces to this day.

I also understood that if some of the persons sitting in the congregation could have heard his story, even if they were not convinced that structural, systemic racism still exists, they would listen because these were his lived experiences, and you can't refute or argue against an actual lived experience. And maybe if they listened, he could have expressed some of what he suffered, which he has never been able to share with a White person. Still, I couldn't say I blamed him for feeling fearful because, as I stated earlier, I have been in some White spaces that were very harmful. But that's what a story does. It takes a person, little more than a caricature or an idea, and turns it into a human being.

THOSE BRAVE FEW

Stories have always been important to people of color. For many years, stories of the past were recited orally. I learned from my grandfather that slave masters used to cut the tongues out of the mouths of those who were enslaved if they posed a threat to organize or speak against harsh treatment, pass along stories, or attempt to read. To know that the tongues of those who were enslaved were cut out for trying to speak up or pass along these important narratives gave me a deeper perspective on why it is important to unearth buried history and include all God's children. Little was documented in writing, causing future generations of people of color to misunderstand their own history.

Fortunately, in every era, there have been a few brave souls who set down their fears and prejudices and waded into the turbulent waters of society to try to calm them. On February 27, 1926, Carter G. Woodson initiated the first sustained effort to expand the study of and scholarship on African American history. It was called Negro History Week. According to the history documented by the NAACP, Woodson faced numerous obstacles after his birth in 1875. His parents were former slaves and illiterate, and he was only able to attend school sporadically. He spent his childhood and teen years working on the family farm and in the West Virginia coal mines. Yet Woodson was eager to learn, and he educated himself on the basic subjects before entering high school at twenty years old. He graduated in less than two years and later became a prominent historian, authoring several books on Black Americans.[10] Woodson believed that the historical contributions of Black people had been "overlooked, ignored, and even suppressed by the writers of history textbooks and the teachers who use them."[11]

Woodson launched Negro History Week in February to co-incide with the birthdays of both Frederick Douglass and Abraham Lincoln. At a time when Black people weren't allowed to use the same bathrooms or sit in the same places on the bus as White people, Woodson felt passionately that the history, heritage, and contributions of Black people should not be lost to posterity.

Before Woodson's efforts, there had been next to nothing, aside from oral histories, available to Black people, or anyone else, to help them understand the true history of Black folks. His Negro History Week later became what we now know as Black History Month, and it has inspired people to learn and teach about Black history year-round. Since 1926, that knowledge has been inscribed in volume after volume. Woodson's legacy has been immeasurable because it is something that Black people have taken pride in 365 days of the year, not just one month. And yet, within our primary learning institutions and even within a large portion of our churches and Bible colleges, this important history is being softened, glazed over, or outright ignored.

In the modern context, I understand how difficult it is for many people who are a part of a majority culture to connect with the full extent of Black history because they do not want to feel responsible for its suppression or oppression. However, it is important to understand how society has been established in a way that elevates the history of White culture and buries and devalues the history of people of color. The racism of today is not so obvious, not so intentional, not so frequent, and not so immersive as it was just a few generations ago. However, that does not mean it is not alive and that we should not call it out every time we see examples of it harming people. In so many ways, it has been inherited without knowledge. Our textbooks teach it. Our churches even contribute to it, perpetuating the fictional image of a pale, White, blue-eyed Jesus. So why, in the times we live in now, when every bit of information we could ever want is at our fingertips, do we still teach and exhibit such obvious and prevailing untruths?

I'm sure I don't know all the reasons, but I do know this: guilt hurts and, most important, the truth hurts. But we cannot heal or stand in solidarity with one another by ignoring these truths. And for those who look across the divide and see the struggles of Black and Brown people in this country and wish they could change a past created by White supremacy, I can't imagine what that must feel like. How tempting must it be to pretend that history never happened or to construct and perpetuate the least painful version of events—which is a part of what it means to create a harmful revisionist history. But we must resist that urge because, as Christina Barland Edmondson notes, "disrupting systems of racial injustice is first and foremost a heart issue."[12]

Instead, if you have been raised in an all-White community or a community that is not Black, it might be helpful to reflect on a few questions. Ask yourself these questions:

- How was Black history taught in my classes?
- What role did Black leaders play in shaping history?
- Did my school teach that it was only European influencers who shaped the economic prosperity we enjoy today?
- Why was Black history not taught in full?
- Why is there so much White backlash when people of color speak about their history to inform the present moment?
- Why did George Floyd's death spark nationwide and worldwide protests?

Asking these tough questions can be difficult, but they lead us down the path of understanding.

EVERYONE HAS A HISTORY

Every time we attempt to distort or alter history, we discredit the effects it has on us. Whitewashing the past only creates an environment for history to repeat itself.

I have a history. You have a history. Every person was given some version of the Talk. For White people, sometimes the Talk is less about what is said and more about what is implied, modeled, or allowed. Maybe Black friends were not allowed; Black churches were something to avoid, and the brown-skinned Jesus was replaced with a pale-faced Savior with blond hair and blue eyes.

I grew up in an all-Black neighborhood, so I did not have any White friends growing up, and that had a tremendous impact on how I saw myself in the world, especially learning how White people saw Black America through the news and what information was avoided in school. And I imagine if people grew up only around others from the same location, it would dramatically shape the way they viewed the world. The Talk isn't just a speech but includes how we have seen those around us live out their lives.

Only a few years before my grandfather was born, D. W. Griffith's *Birth of a Nation* debuted on the silver screen. It was the first movie that held racism at its core that was played in the White House. This was the first time blackface had been used in a motion picture, and the film portrayed Black people as inferior creatures, barely above beasts. That kind of visual rhetoric assigned to an entire segment of society was damaging, not only for that era's Black people but for the generations that were raised by the people who bore that pain. Imagery is powerful because it perpetuates harmful narratives. It made it that much harder for Black men and women to be viewed as equals, on top of what the enslavement period did. The Bible tells us that we are God's creation and God's special workmanship. We are all God's children, and it is important for us to understand the worth and value of each person and their historical shaping.

Everyone has a past to unpack and understand. What is your history? What conversations did you have as a child that shaped the way you think today about race? How did you see BIPOC groups treated in your community? What writers, speakers, and political leaders influence your thinking? What is the lens through which you view society? All these factors play a role in shaping how you view the world and those you wish to stand in solidarity with.

APPLICATION

If you are pondering any of my words in depth, here is my challenge to you as we embark on the rest of these chapters. I challenge you to do some deep introspection as to what version of the Talk you heard growing up, whether in words or deeds, and sit with those memories. Sit with them against the backdrop of truths you may be unearthing from hearing parts of history that might have been kept from you. Before you do anything, you must first evaluate the history you've been taught, whether consciously or subconsciously, and how it has impacted the way you see others.

When you see a Black person or a person of color, ask yourself a few questions:

- Do I have an automatic response?
- Am I afraid or disgusted, or do I feel guilty?
- Do I smile a little wider, trying to show the other person I "don't see color"?

Ask yourself, *Where does this framing come from?* The answer might be obvious, or it might not. You might have to search for it deep within yourself or within your past, but finding it is the first step toward understanding. Before I understood my grandfather's past, I did not see my own world clearly. But when I entered his world, which is connected to the history of my ancestors, my world opened up. When we choose to discover the history of another person or explore our own historical shaping, we can truly see the people standing right before our eyes, and thus understand our own shaping—and that honors God.

A HISTORY
FEW WANTED
TO UNDERSTAND

The simultaneous peak of both racial tensions and Covid-19 in the United States was one of the hardest moments of my life. When protests broke out across the country and people were stuck at home, forced to pay attention to clear disparities, Black people experienced immense racialized trauma from seeing the killings of other Black people plastered all over national television. While we struggled deeply with loss and grief, White people made posts on social media excusing those killings like we were supposed to brush them under a rug of inaction. At the same time, there were many White churches that, for the first time, really started to understand they could no longer sit silently while watching yet another Black person have their life taken by law enforcement. Covid-19 created a moment of reckoning in which everyone had to pause and sit with injustices that had been ignored for too long.

Suddenly, there was more of an interest in racial justice and racial healing than usual, and many churches started conversations about race for the first time. Leaders of White congregations scrambled to figure out how to respond to what had happened to George Floyd. There it was, seared in our minds: the image of Floyd with a White police officer's knee pressed against his neck and headlines about other people whose lives were taken. I still cannot unsee this video and image in my mind. Within hours of the video of the officer with his knee pressed against George Floyd's neck going viral and being shown nationally all over the news, a dozen White pastors had reached out and asked me to review their church statements on racial justice, look over sermon manuscripts, or prerecord a word of encouragement to their churches.

"Should I say this?" one friend texted. "I emailed my sermon notes. Could you read my introduction?" another one asked. And on and on—even White pastors I did not know who had followed me on social media for some time reached out to me for comment.

Part of me rejoiced. I have always loved educating others on racial justice and was thankful for this sudden eagerness to learn. But there was another part of me, a large part, that was frustrated, sorrowful, and even full of grief and sadness. It was not only a heavy burden to experience racial trauma from the imagery of Floyd's murder, it was equally tough to face the barrage of questions from White pastors because it meant they had largely overlooked racism or injustice on their church platforms. Why had it taken so long for these leaders to address this subject in their services when Black congregations had been speaking about it for years? Although I respected some of these leaders' desire to be sensitive in the messages they shared, I also felt as if I were being asked to provide a cheat sheet for a racial justice quiz to those who didn't want to study. It was as though they were saying, "Terence, just help me get through this crisis so we can go back to not talking about it again!"

Moreover, the weight I felt was intense. Every morning, from the Ahmaud Arbery shooting in February until long after Floyd's murder in May, I woke up with a sense of heaviness, which only intensified when we heard of the passing of Breonna Taylor. The day after Arbery was killed, I was jogging through a predominately White neighborhood when, all of a sudden, I was gripped by fear. My heart started racing, my palms became sweaty, and I struggled to keep it together. Some of my Black friends told me of similar fears and sent me texts: "I'm afraid to leave my house"; "Are we safe anywhere?"; "I'm completely exhausted." Other Black people took to social media to talk about the realities of what Black people go through when we see images of pain on television.

If you are White, it may be difficult for you to fully understand this feeling, but if I could paint a picture for you about how racialized trauma feels, it's a bit like thinking you're going to be in a horrible car accident. You're speeding down an icy highway when suddenly a semi whips in front of you, almost hitting your vehicle, but somehow you avoid an accident. You regain control of the wheel and pull over to the side of the road, realizing how awful the situation was and how close you came to death. Soon you are back to driving, but the anxiety and fear do not leave your body right away. You feel the horror from the almost fatal accident that took place. At the same time, relief washes over you that your life was spared, followed by an increase in heartrate.

Although this is not physically what takes place with racial trauma, the anxiety, emotions, and impact are just as intense. In the back of our minds, whenever we see a Black boy or girl killed, the thought that pops into our heads is, *That could have been me.*

When Floyd died, there was already a great deal on my plate. Our nation was in the midst of a pandemic, and my Atlanta-based organization was attempting to help unhoused communities without basic sanitation through this challenging time. My staff and I were on the frontlines fighting beside our unhoused neighbors to help them remain safe from Covid-19. I worked around the clock to install handwashing stations for members of the unhoused community and followed this up with media interviews to spread the word. There was so much to do. In fact, from the moment they announced that Covid-19 was a threat until I sat down to write these words, I didn't come off the frontlines.

Suddenly, added to this load was the heartbreak of the Black community coupled with the eagerness of White churches to make sense of it all. I was facing an awkward tension whereby pastors wanted me to address their churches but to do so in a manner that was palatable for their White congregations.

FAILURE TO UNDERSTAND THE PAST
CAUSES PAIN IN THE PRESENT

The fall of 2020 offered little reprieve. On September 20, my wife and I received news that her sister's husband had passed away from Covid-19, leaving behind his wife and three kids. Once again, grief swept through our home. Our brother had passed while on a ventilator. His children had to say their goodbyes over a laptop, and at the same time I started to see many White friends post about their freedom being taken away because "Covid is a hoax," like one person said. We grappled with all that was going on and with the added weight of supporting my wife's sister during this heartbreaking time.

As fate would have it, this happened to be a presidential election year, and many White people I knew were concerned the leader they revered would no longer be in office. Now, I'm a firm believer in collaboration. I work with people from all walks of life. Love Beyond Walls is an organization whose tagline is "Movement of Doers." Many of my friends come from various social backgrounds, and I prefer to keep it that way. But unless you are Black or Brown, it is difficult to put into words the sheer weight of the verbal abuse that emerged from the Trump administration. This president's words were so disruptive on television and through social media, even Twitter decided to permanently ban his account because of hurtful things he would say through tweets that were divisive. NPR covered the removal of his account, stating that Twitter did this because his words were at risk of inciting violence among those who held racial hatred in their hearts.[1] And, to add insult to injury, many folks excused this behavior that they would not tolerate from anyone else. It wasn't just the hurtful tweets. Trump supporters I had known for years suddenly felt emboldened to make some of the most hurtful, racist statements I had ever heard or read. They were taking their cues from the president, who had little regard for how he treated persons or those whom he did not agree with or like. In an article titled "The Ever-Growing List of Racist Rants," Andrea González-Ramírez documented a series of actual racialized tweets Trump wrote that were extremely harmful.[2] They ranged from tweets about immigrants, Muslims, Black people, Asian Americans, Mexican people, Native Americans, Jewish people, and Puerto Ricans, to White nationalists, and more. For the sake of keeping the list short, check out some of the things González-Ramírez documented aimed toward Black people:

- In October 2019, Trump called the impeachment inquiry against him a "lynching," comparing a constitutionally sanctioned process to the extrajudicial murders of Black Americans following the Civil War. According to the NAACP, there were 4,743 recorded lynchings between

1882 and 1968. Roughly three-quarters of the victims were African American, and lynching was used as a weapon to terrorize the Black community.

- In May 2020, Trump took to Twitter to express his displeasure with the antiracism protests around the country following the killings of Floyd and other Black Americans. "These THUGS are dishonoring the memory of George Floyd, and I won't let that happen. Just spoke to Governor Tim Walz and told him that the military is with him all the way," he wrote. "Any difficulty and we will assume control but, when the looting starts, the shooting starts." The phrase "when the looting starts, the shooting starts" has a racist history, being used before by a segregationist politician and a White police chief in response to civil unrest. Twitter placed a warning on the tweet, saying it "violated the Twitter Rules about glorifying violence."

- In June 2020, Trump called antiracism protesters "looters, thugs" and "others [sic] forms of lowlife & scum" on Twitter. Later that month, at a campaign rally in Tulsa, Oklahoma, he called demonstrators in the city "thugs," even though police reports said protests in the city had been peaceful.[3]

The tweets were so outrageous that they were even in support of people who openly identified as White nationalists. González-Ramírez went on to document these tweets:

August 2017: Following the Unite the Right white nationalist rally in Charlottesville, Virginia, that led to the murder of counterprotester Heather Heyer, Trump refused to condemn the right-wing marchers. Instead, he insisted that "many sides" and "both sides" were to blame for the day's violence. Trump also said that the white nationalist groups included "some very fine people."

When Joe Biden was elected president, there was a reason CNN's Van Jones, a Black man and parent, described it as a "good day." As he shared, George Floyd's words "I can't breathe" represented the feelings of many people during the Trump presidency.[4] In no way am I comparing the politics of Trump and Biden, but I do want to draw a comparison in the way many people in society felt underneath the forty-fifth administration and leadership that in many ways was overwhelming for women, Black and Brown people, and marginalized communities.

It's hard to articulate the many comments I received as a Black man during this time. But no conversation would be more painful than the one I had with a couple who once supported our organization. The week after my brother-in-law's death, they asked if they could call to pray with my wife and me over the phone. Thankful for their support, I agreed.

Five minutes into our conversation, the topic shifted to politics. They stopped talking about our grief and began talking about everything President Trump was going through, "because he is being blamed for Covid" they said, and completely ignored the fact that we had just lost a loved one to Covid-19. We were devastated. They spoke about how Covid was not his fault and how he was receiving unfair criticism in the media. It felt like their conversation and prayers were not about our pain but had an underlying focus on prayers for our nation that somehow God would intervene, and that President Trump would be protected. We could not believe what we were hearing on the other end of the phone.

As they prayed, I glanced over at my wife. Tears streamed down her face, and I knew they were not tears of gratitude, but tears of pain that a couple who professed to love and serve Jesus would speak to us this way in our darkest hour of tragedy and need. What hurt the most was the sheer insensitivity of it all. In that moment, we felt that our grief had to be placed on hold in the midst of political grievances with us. It was not Jesus at all.

This story is common among countless Black Christians during those months after Floyd's death. I remember numerous times speaking up about racial justice to add to the conversation about validating Black worth. Afterward, I would be bombarded with hate messages, nasty comments on social profiles, gaslighting, and microaggressions. It was as if those of us who were experiencing pain were not being heard. It was inattentional blindness overload. The justifications for Floyd's death seemed endless and drove home the point that sometimes a Black man dies two deaths. The first is his actual death at the hands of law enforcement officers, and the second is when others assassinate his character now that he is unable to defend himself.

Sadly, this wasn't the first time I had encountered these types of conversations from my White brothers and sisters who professed to follow Jesus. I was not surprised because I had been here before in my Christian journey.

IT'S HARD TO HEAR WHAT ISN'T SEEN

I heard these conversations during my time in Bible college in my early twenties. The Bible college was predominately White, and as a Black man—one of maybe four in the entire school—it was hard walking in the buildings and seeing pictures of a blond-haired, blue-eyed White person who was supposed to be Jesus. It was even harder learning the Scriptures in a way that promoted the same ideology. Many of the persons who led revivals in the United States and the theology scholars we read were slave owners, as Tisby uncovered in his brilliant book *The Color of Compromise*. There would be times in class where I would mention Black scholars, Black-led churches, and Black Christian leaders, and the professors would dismiss them in a subtly

demeaning way. Classes on worship equated vibrant expressions of worship in the Black church with a lack of substance.

The message was clear. Sure, Black Christians love and serve
Jesus, but they are on the "low church" end of the spectrum.
White students upheld these ideologies with social and political rhetoric, and this attitude pervades many Christian
circles today. For example, before going on staff at a White
church, I was asked to jump through a series of hoops other
candidates, who were White, did not face. They asked me to
send a recording of my preaching, write a sermon, and be
quizzed before I could even preach to the congregation. When
I spoke, I was the first Black person to ever preach in this particular church. It was a monolithic approach that was skeptical
of BIPOC people, individuals who brought their unique gifts
to the table and understood the Scriptures related to our
struggles and experiences in this country. I noticed this skep-
ticism whenever I applied to be a pastor at predominantly
White churches. While my White colleagues, many of whom
had fewer credentials than I did, were asked to submit a simple
résumé, I was forced to go through an entire vetting process to
ensure that my theological beliefs were sound—or that I did
not come across too Black, whatever that means. It was tough,
and it reminded me of the pain I felt when wanting to understand both my history as a Black person and the unique contributions of our blackness in the expression of church.

The theological training I received in Bible college indirectly
attempted to make me feel as if blackness and Black people
were a mistake, and there were no Black scholars to study in
the theological advancement of the text. This was never ver-
bally said out loud, but it happened subtly in the way texts
were discussed, Black scholars were talked about in harmful,
heretical ways, and the way inclusion was lacking and not happening in those spaces and classrooms. Even the evangelical

dictionaries we used labeled Black scholars like James Cone and Howard Thurman as heretical. Later, I learned that this was a lie, but during those confusing years I often asked myself, *Will Black people ever be able to communicate for God in a way that is accepted widely in the United States? Or will there always be pushback when a Black person provides scholarship that affirms our blackness through a different lens?*

This was painful for me, as I had already wrestled with not having access to the full Black history in school, and now I found myself in a predominantly White college hearing these things again. *How could this be happening in Bible college?* I asked myself many times. I was new to Christianity, and I thought God was for all God's children, so I struggled with understanding why this was happening.

Impostor syndrome greeted me every time I walked into class, and there were days I literally had to give myself a talking to in order to remind myself that I am also part of God's family. I felt like an outsider when I was in class and constantly wrestled with my Black identity in this White theological setting. I knew this was not the God I had signed up to worship and follow.

Church, however, was a different story during my development and was a constant contrast to the college I attended. While in Bible college, I attended a Black congregation, and I felt like I fit in because I had representation all around me. I could be myself, and that was enough. My blackness was understood and celebrated. In the back of my mind, however, I could not understand this disconnect. Both the Bible college and my church worshiped the same God, yet there was a vast difference in the way he was depicted.

When Black History Month came around in February, my church took the time to celebrate. People dressed in African garb, sermons addressed the struggles Black people everywhere faced, and the congregation took action steps to help marginalized people. But my Bible college did nothing. There were no school-sponsored events or presentations on this topic, and professors avoided it altogether. I sat in class shifting uneasily between anger and sadness. I could not understand how a topic so important in one culture could be so completely ignored and buried in another.

WHY IT'S IMPORTANT TO SEE COLOR

Confused, I asked one of my White friends to explain why Black History Month was avoided as a topic. His response was like that of his colleagues. "I don't see color," he replied, delivering this line as if it were a mic-drop moment.

To him, it was a no-brainer. What my friend failed to realize is that when Black and Brown people hear the words "I don't see color," what we really hear is that our color, that which makes us who we are, can be easily dismissed. It tells us that how God created us is somehow invalid and that only without color are we worthy to be recognized and valued.

Every single time a White brother or sister has said this to me, it has made me feel the weight of the mistreatment and suffering my ancestors went through. Imagine telling someone who wakes up Black every single day that they live in a society that doesn't see color—when every experience they have suggests otherwise! And herein lies the problem. Because many White Christians have not witnessed racial injustice firsthand, they feel no need to discuss the topic. The dialogue tends to go something like this: Yes, we know a lot of bad things happened in the past. That's terrible, but every nation has its blind spots. Fortunately, America is different, and we have moved past all that. Sure, some people have certain advantages, but if you work hard enough and pull yourself up by your bootstraps, you should be able to get along just fine!

And for many, the narrative ends there.

Why talk about George Floyd, Ahmaud Arbery, Breonna Taylor, and so many others who have lost their lives at the hands of the racially violent? What good does it do to bring up "outlier cases" that do not represent what most of the population believes? Doesn't this move our nation backward? Shouldn't colorblindness be the goal of every American? Wasn't that what MLK and others in the civil rights movement fought to accomplish?

This is something of a hot-button topic with me because I am bothered when I hear public figures or politicians quote King and then institute racist agendas that discriminate against the very people he sought to protect. As Esau Mc-Caulley points out, "King's point was never that ethnicity and culture are irrelevant, but that they should not be the cause of discrimination." And McCaulley rightly goes on to note that "King often called on African Americans to take pride in their culture and heritage."[5]

Nowhere in Scripture does God present colorblindness as the ideal for his followers. In fact, the opposite is true. If there were ever a place this might be a reality, it would be in heaven. But in John's vision in Revelation 7:9, he looks and sees a "great multitude that no one could count, from every nation, tribe, people and language, standing before the throne and before the Lamb." Unfortunately, in some White Christians' quests to avoid seeing color, they have become blind to the differences and beauties that make others unique.

To say to a Black person "I don't see your color" is not only an obvious misstatement of fact, but a willful decision to ignore what makes them who they are. When someone says this to me, I hear them say they do not see the generations of injustice and the impact they have had on Black lives today.

To put it another way, one of the basic constructs of good exegesis is understanding the context of Scripture. You do not open the Bible and start speaking from Joel 2 without describing the backstory of the northern kingdom of Israel and the southern kingdom of Judah. It's impossible to celebrate the Israelites' journey into Canaan without discussing their slavery in Egypt. In fact, the entire message of the cross makes little sense without the historical context of the children of Israel. Only if you acknowledge the Jewish people's years of captivity and longing for a Savior does the cross make sense. To make this connection does not somehow diminish the power of the cross. It emphasizes it. Only then do we behold the larger picture of God's work in human history. It makes books like the four Gospels, Acts, and Romans come alive.

When my White peers tell me they do not see color, I know they are not trying to be hurtful or intentionally callous. Rather, they are responding through the lens of their own limited experience. Because their upbringing differs greatly from mine, they see my reality in a different light. They did not grow up in the Black community, attend a Black church, or sit down beside Black grandparents—like my grandfather.

Yet this lack of understanding can cause unspeakable division. Ignoring a person's historical shaping is just like pushing someone away intentionally; there is no close connection without it, and the relationship will always remain surface-level.

THE GREAT DIVIDE BETWEEN WHITE AND BLACK CHRISTIANS

After Bible college, I worked as an itinerant minister. This involved going from place to place and serving whatever ministry-based needs I found. Invitations tended to involve requests to address youth and young adult crowds at Black churches, Latinx churches, African churches, and some White churches. I often wondered why the expressions of faith were so different. I especially noticed vast differences between Black churches and White churches when I visited to preach. The worship was different; often, the sermon content was different; the prayers against injustice were different, and the concerns with disparities were different.

Black churches had a strong leaning toward social justice and incorporated justice in liturgy and talked about issues in society, stemming back to the civil rights era when Black churches became meeting spaces in which to plan, organize, and fight systematic injustice with the help of faith. The White churches I spoke at, however, left out matters of injustice in worship and did not address systemic issues as a part of the gospel because they are not personally affected by these things on a daily basis.

A little while after college, I found a second pastorship, which provided more stability. This new church was a little diverse, giving me the impression it was an authentic, multiethnic church. However, I soon learned the difference between a multiethnic church and a White church with a multiethnic congregation.

My time as a pastor in the predominantly White-led church taught me many lessons. One of them was that if the lead pastor was White, I had to keep my blackness out of my messages. I was never allowed to speak with the fullness of my personality. It's worth noting that this is a common theme with many Black communicators today. Whenever they speak at White churches, they feel the need to change their style and cadence to make their message more palatable. In other words, they must come across as less "Black." In addition, Black leaders were seen as a rarity. To many of my White colleagues, I was an outlier, someone who had defied the norms of Black culture—rather than recognizing that Black culture is valuable.

In Black churches there was always an openness about the struggles we faced as a community. If a tragic event rocked the Black community, we talked about it on Sunday. We prayed prayers of lament, and the liturgy focused on violence. We took a public theological stand regarding what God had to say about the current climate.

This White-led church was different. Whenever a crisis in the Black community occurred, I received little sympathy. Instead, I was often cornered with questions such as, "Why are all these things happening?" as though I were to blame. I would hear dismissive language such as, "So many Black people are doing well. What's the problem?" There was no desire to understand how a person of color felt when a member of their community suffered loss.

Some of this boils down to tradition and expression of worship, while some of it is influenced by White supremacy. There were times when it felt like there was an intense focus on personal faith in the predominately White-led church at the expense of their public faith, and it was hard being in a space where the people around me focused more on their faith and very little on ways they could combat injustices that plagued other parts of the family of God.

HEALING INCLUDES THOSE IN POWER

If you are White, you might think to yourself, *Terence, this conversation feels a bit lopsided. It seems like you go out of your way to point out the problems in White churches while ignoring the issues in Black churches.* I hear you, and I would be the first to point out that I have had more than a few White professors and colleagues over the years that I learned from and from whom I have gleaned support and encouragement.

However, the reason my appeal might seem tilted is because the conversation itself rests on a slanted foundation. For example, if I speak to a room of White people and ask them to name some of the ways Black people have been marginalized, I receive a series of quick responses: "slavery," "slave patrolling," "Jim Crow," "Black shootings," "segregation," "the War on Drugs," "mandatory minimums," and so forth.

When I flip the question and ask for ways Black people have historically discriminated against White people, the room grows quiet. (When I mention this discrimination, I am talking about having the power to actually do structural and systemic harm to those who are predominantly White.) The reason for this quiet can be summarized in a single word: power. Like it or not, in many social, political, and religious communities, White people have held the power in the United States and in many ways still do hold that power. If racial healing is to occur, it will require confronting this truth and laying that power down. That means White pastors treating their Black brothers and sisters as equals, and centering BIPOC people and their voices, experiences, and histories that have helped shape this country. It means refusing to reframe the conversation in a way that appeals to White audiences. And it means being true to the narratives that are often overlooked by the dominant narratives.

Public conversations and panel discussions at churches are all very well. Unfortunately, the power dynamic of these conversations is often tilted. How often have we seen racial reconciliation conversations happen when a White leader invites a Black or Brown person to speak on their terms, using language that makes their congregations comfortable? I have been a part of these conversations, and I cannot even begin to express the emotional trauma I have carried away from them. This needs to change. When we look at the New Testament and the gap between Jewish and Gentile believers, it was the gospel that bridged that gap. And when leaders like Peter stumbled, it was others like Paul who stepped up and put them back on the right path, and this is what needs to happen in churches today: confronting what is right before our eyes in a way that is healthy.

MEETING PEOPLE WHERE THEY ARE

As someone who speaks out against social, economic, and racial injustice, I am used to discussing topics that make others feel uncomfortable. But understanding these topics only comes through meeting people where they are.

Several years ago, I spent a week living on the streets among those experiencing homelessness in Atlanta, and on another occasion, my family allowed me to live on the streets for a month and a week. Even though I had experienced home-lessness, this time I chose to live unhoused to advocate on behalf of the unhoused to get them access to more resources in the city. I entered this time with some trepidation, scarcely sleeping a wink the night before. Part of me knew what to expect: cold nights with little food or other resources at my disposal. That said, I was unprepared for the conversations and public stigmatization I experienced. Businesspeople who would have previously said "Good morning" to me suddenly crossed the street to steer clear of me and my new friends.

Both experiences combined were a month and a half, and they both changed me. I wasn't off in an ivory tower, philoso-phizing about how to end homelessness in Atlanta. Instead, I went to where the people were. I lived life with them. I listened to their concerns and experienced their pain. My time among those experiencing homelessness shifted my viewpoint more than any conversation could.

Although class and race are different, in both realms there is something life changing about being close to someone's unique life experience or standing with people in solidarity. It would be life changing for the White church to get close to matters of racial justice. If you want to be part of the healing process in the church, start by being comfortable with awkward conversations.

Opening yourself up to the hurts of others, hearing their story and what it's like to walk in their shoes, is not only what changes us but also what starts us on a path of doing the real work. We live in a time in which it is critical not to rely on hearsay about a community, but to get to know that community, particularly those who are hurting, and feel their pain. In doing this we come to understand that each one of God's children has a unique story.

If we are committed to practicing solidarity and antiracism, this is the work we must do. In fact, being a faithful antiracist means living, as Dr. Christina Edmondson says, and "work[ing] against the forces that sustain racism."[6] Working against racism isn't like chopping down a tree, where one focused act of exertion can bring an entire structure to its knees. Instead, being a faithful antiracist is more like being a vigilant gardener. It's a commitment to careful nurturing and a daily determination to remove any weeds that might rear their ugly heads.

The way we understand someone's historical shaping is by decentering ourselves and remembering the universe does not revolve around us. It's about not allowing our narrative to dominate space where someone else's storyline or history becomes a footnote. It's learning how to be with people and be immersed in their lives so we can learn a new narrative.

APPLICATION

Have you ever felt like someone did not understand your story? Is there a part of your life you feel others cannot comprehend? Consider how this makes you feel. If you have gone through the pain of a relationship breakup, think of some of the hurtful comments others might have made about you. Or if you grew up with a troubled past, think about how it makes you feel when others make assumptions about your background. These can be painful, and no doubt you've said to yourself a time or two, *If they only knew my story!*

With these thoughts in mind, ask yourself how you might channel your past hurt to better learn the stories of Black people or people of color in this country. A large part of antiracist work is decentering oneself to understand the perspective of another, especially if you are in a place of power and privilege. What if tomorrow, the next day, or this week, you made an intentional effort to dig beneath the surface and understand the history of one of God's children who looks a little different from you? Race is a big topic, and structural institutional racism can feel like it's too overwhelming to be able to make a difference. But you have the power to start with one person. Remember, Jesus cared for all, but he told a story of a shepherd that left the ninety-nine sheep for the one. Start with one, and slowly build your capacity to take in more and learn more. Whose story will you hear?

CHAPTER **THREE**

GOD IS
JUSTICE

In some White evangelical church settings, like the one in which I served, it's common to hear messages that contradict one another. On one hand, we hear sermons about God being a healer, a God who redeems, and One who empowers people to get back up after tragedy, leveraging the gospel to do so. On the other hand, that same rhetoric isn't always used where systemic injustice is causing all types of pain and social harm for Black and Brown people. One message is of hope while the other is of silence.

Many times, White evangelical spaces are quiet when injustices cause trauma, pain, and terror in Black communities, which leaves many Black people and people of color asking where the messages are about God's justice, healing, and presence after tragedy. In *My Grandmother's Hands*, Resmaa Menakem writes, "Trauma is not a flaw or a weakness. It is a highly effective tool of safety and survival. Trauma is also not an event. Trauma is the body's protective response to an event—or a series of events—that it perceives as potentially dangerous."[1] Menakem speaks about trauma as something that is not uncommon and separate from reality, but sometimes churches act as though the opposite is true.

I remember vividly when I experienced this disassociation from a White pastor in a predominately White church space. On July 6, 2016, Philando Castile, a thirty-two-year-old Black male, was shot dead by a Minnesota police officer. Audiotapes revealed that within forty seconds of police approaching the vehicle Castile admitted that he was carrying a concealed weapon with a permit. Shortly after this revelation, Officer Jeronimo Yanez opened fire, mistakenly believing Castile was reaching for his firearm. Castile died minutes later, uttering the words, "I wasn't reaching."[2]

In the aftermath of this incident and the ensuing nationwide protests, the pastor of the White church where I was on staff asked me to speak about this tragedy to our congregation on Sunday. His request felt more like a demand, and he didn't even pause to ask if I was okay after seeing Castile's bloody white shirt while his daughter sat in the backseat and watched the whole thing. I was so triggered, I could barely speak. I was in shock mainly because Castile's child was in the backseat, and I am a Black man that had young children at the time. It was gut-wrenching, because I, like many other Black men, saw part of ourselves through Castile's interaction with the police officer.

Let's pause for a moment. Think about what I carried in my body watching this play out on social media and television and holding my young Black children. It was frightening and, moreover, overwhelming not to be acknowledged. The Bible says that we are supposed to "bear one another's burdens."

Because I was the only Black pastor on staff, he saw me as the obvious voice to speak to the shame and guilt people were feeling.[3] This is a huge no-no. Even if the person who was murdered is not our own family member or friend, a part of us sees ourselves not only through the lens of history and what our people have endured but also in the collective pain that we experience day in and day out when we see those like us murdered, mistreated, or experiencing injustice. After we experience any form of racial trauma, Black people carry that trauma in our bodies.

I wish the pastor had given me that Sunday to rest and lament privately. But instead he urged me to give a clear message. I was to avoid speaking about social justice and focus instead on the nature of God's forgiveness and how we could love those who wronged us. I was expected to put a Band-Aid solution on a deep-seated problem.

This tragedy occurred on the heels of Alton Sterling's death at the hands of law enforcement, so the pain I felt during this season was intense. Imagine the back-to-back trauma Black people carried at that time in our bodies, and I shared this hurt with the pastor I was serving with at the time, but my grief went unheard and overlooked.

Deep down, his actions showed me that the only reason I had been hired was because of my skin color, not because I actually had something meaningful to say that would help to change the way that we spoke about God, injustice, racial healing, and solidarity. The church wanted a well-spoken Black man to exhibit diversity to its church community and to expand its sphere of influence. As I spoke with the pastor, what troubled me was his lack of empathy for the cause he wanted to address. He wanted history buried under the guise of false forgiveness and togetherness. He wasn't approaching this tragedy from a place of lament; rather, he thought it was an opportunity to grow the congregation to attract more Black people and people of color, as he openly told me in a conversation at a later date.

What came as a result of the tragedy was a panel discussion with two White congregants and me casually talking about tragic injustices that the Black community was not only facing but also deeply grieving. Before the panel started, I sat behind the stage curtain and listened to the worship band play, and anxiety and fear washed over me. I wished I could have had a Sunday to breathe and not have to do the work of trying to make people feel better. The pain of the situation was so great that sharing words could not assuage the heaviness that I and others in the church were feeling. But there was also this weird pressure from the pastor to represent Black America. He wanted me to offer some hope toward racial reconciliation and, as happens in many White evangelical churches, move forward.

At several points during this discussion, I looked down and noticed the few Black faces in attendance, and I could tell they sensed my pain, and I could see their pain. I could see how being in the space alone was heavy and how they shared my grief. There were a few who walked up to me with genuine concerns after the panel, but others brushed off the words I communicated in church because it had things to do with buried history. Looking back, I do not blame myself or feel bad; rather, that experience has given me the ability to write these words. I write this book as a whole person who cares about how the church must be better, do better, and stop the pain and hurt it is causing to many Black people and people of color.

That morning, I felt like a sacrificial scapegoat in a heavy conversation on race, a feeling many Black people and people of color have in similar settings where they are the minority. The pastor used the human tragedy of a Black body to tug at the heartstrings of the congregants in an attempt to grow the church.[4] It was a gross malpractice of faith at best. His actions were in stark contrast to what took place at the historically Black congregation where I pastored. For the first time I realized that the entire discussion of racial reconciliation was premature and, in fact, impossible to comprehend without an adequate understanding of justice.

A GOD OF JUSTICE

The word *justice* appears hundreds of times in the Bible. Dr. Mae Cannon shows in *Social Justice Handbook* that there are references to justice throughout Scripture. In the Old Testament, the word *justice* means "right action," but it does not stop there. *Justice* and *righteousness* work hand in hand with one another. While justice is about "right action," righteousness is about "being of pure heart," which moves us closer to God's character. Cannon states that "justice is the expression of God's righteousness through right action. When justice completely exists on this earth, everything will be the way that God indented it to be."[5] Micah 6:8 states, "He has shown you, O mortal, what is good. And what does the LORD require of you? To act justly and to love mercy and to walk humbly with your God."

Unfortunately, many Christians in the evangelical community have a skewed understanding of *justice*. When they hear this word they are quick to latch on to a specific cause or agenda, leaving some to view social justice as heretical. When asked whether the word *justice* should be preceded by *social*, retired Methodist minister J. Philip Wogaman responds, "Perhaps not. But since justice is so often taken at the narrower, more individualist sense of giving people what they earn or deserve, the adjective social is a reminder that justice is about community."[6] Justice and community are intertwined.

At its core, biblical justice is about making wrongs right. It's looking at something that has been shattered and offering solutions to piece it back together. God's justice is supreme. God looks at a broken world where there is so much wrong and promises to make it right in the new earth and new heaven. Part of bringing heaven to earth is initiating this justice and ensuring that those who have been wronged by injustice get a chance to experience life-giving justice when things are made right for them. No, this does not mean replacing God or forming our own version of heaven on earth, but it also does not mean that we should allow those who are marginalized by injustice to suffer. God is the ultimate judge, and there are some wrongs that will only be made right after this life is over, but part of having a strong theology of justice is recognizing that our lives play a small part in bringing God's justice to earth.

During my undergraduate studies, the hardest class for me to grasp was systematic theology, as I struggled to understand how a benevolent God could allow evil in the world. I learned there are various forms of natural evil, such as earthquakes and diseases. And then there is general evil, which is generated by a sinful person making horrible decisions that affect the lives of others. A quick scan of history reveals that the evil and unjust intentions of one individual can bring untold devastation to the world. Genghis Khan was responsible for the death of over forty million people in the Mongol Empire. Joseph Stalin murdered twenty million Russians. Mao Zedong instigated the death of nearly fifty million Chinese people. Adolf Hitler ordered the death of millions of Jews. European slave traders were responsible for the death of nearly two million slaves during the transatlantic slave trade. Currently Vladimir Putin is killing innocent families, children, and anyone else in Ukraine who resists the Russian army.

Some evangelical communities struggle to grasp the racial injustice happening right in their backyards or in their neighborhoods. During my time as a pastor in this predominantly

White congregation, there seemed to be a disconnect between the messages preached on Sundays and the injustice that plagued communities in our front and backyard throughout the week. We would sing about the goodness of God, but I would see people in the congregation drive past neighborhoods that were in dire need of help. It's like the meme that says sometimes evangelicals fly overseas to take pictures with Black and Brown people and miss opportunities to right the wrongs that Black people face right around them. Instead of talking about the neighborhoods in a way that moved us to show up with God's love and stand in solidarity with those who are oppressed, there was often a disdain for poor folks. This stemmed from a weak public theology of justice. For example, when there was an instance of police brutality in our community, the common response from those in our church was to speak up and say things like "Blue Lives Matter," or "All Lives Matter." I remember a Black police officer in the church stating that once he took off his uniform and drove in predominately White areas, he was still Black and afraid for his life, and when he was pulled over a few times by law enforcement himself, he still had the same shock and chills that all Black men face. As for the homelessness crisis, little was said about politicians who backed laws that made it more difficult for the unhoused population to survive.

A public theology of social justice is therefore critical. It affirms what we believe God says about any crisis we face and about what plagues the live of Black and Brown people every single day. Our gospel is not a social gospel, but it is social because it involves people. It has the power to affect people in their social contexts, offering good news for their social problems. What does God say about putting people in cages? What does he say about gun violence? War? The death penalty? What does he say about systemic injustice? A public theology asks, What does God have to say about the evil, injustice, and oppression that is happening in our world in real time? It is exegeting the cultural climate and giving understanding of what God has to say about what we find there.

Unfortunately, when it comes to systemic social injustice against Black people in America, the common response among some Christian leaders is to navigate their way through the crisis as quickly as possible while never addressing the root causes of the problem. Some fear the potential personal consequences of speaking out against the issues, and others don't concern themselves with such issues at all. They make the decision to remove themselves from the weight this injustice carries, which has its own consequences. As Henri Nouwen writes, "Our efforts to disconnect ourselves from our own suffering end up disconnecting our suffering from God's suffering for us."[7]

At the historically Black church where I served as the pastor of social justice and witness, I was given the space to lament, share my frustrations, and talk about what it meant to embody racial justice and take a stand against the evils of poverty, militarism, and anything that oppresses God's children. At the predominately White church, we went straight to talking about forgiveness and racial reconciliation. But as Jemar Tisby rightly asks, "If different races of people have never had conciliation how can they have re-conciliation?"[8]

Before speaking about racial reconciliation, we must first discuss solidarity and justice.

SOLIDARITY LEADS TO JUSTICE

In a recent study, the Barna Group found "a significant increase in the percentage of practicing Christians who say race is 'not at all' a problem in the United States (19 percent, up from 11 percent in 2019)."[9]

Racial justice and racial reconciliation are two distinct conversations that many White Christians conflate into one. The leap straight to racial reconciliation leaves out how a White supremacist system created the oppressive structures that disadvantage many people of color today. Just as an enslaved army cannot forgive its way out of captivity, a culturally oppressed people cannot forgive its way out of oppression. It must be liberated.

Racial injustice cannot be solved through peace, unity, and racial reconciliation conversations. We must deploy thoughtful justice, love, mercy, and solidarity as well. Racial solidarity is a commitment to stand with Black people and persons of color against injustice. The church holds an advantage in the conversation about racial justice and racial solidarity because it can embody both to achieve liberation and a sense of togetherness. The church universal has every nation, tongue, and tribe in it, as John writes in the book of Revelation. We need to see the gospel as empowering us to forgive one another and also pushing us to show up like Jesus on the front lines with good news for the poor, weary, and oppressed.

Jesus said, "The Spirit of the Lord is on me, because he has anointed me to proclaim good news to the poor. He has sent me to proclaim freedom for the prisoners and recovery of sight for the blind, to set the oppressed free" (Luke 4:18). Imagine if the church modeled how to be about both forgiveness and liberation of the oppressed. It was the great Howard Thurman in *Jesus and the Disinherited* who reminds us that Jesus himself identified with those who were minorities or under oppression.[10]

Racial reconciliation must be preceded by racial justice. For racial justice to be achieved, White people who care about the injustices faced by BIPOC persons must learn what it means to stand in solidarity with their BIPOC brothers and sisters. Talk of reconciliation without any reference to solidarity and justice to correct the systems that created the injustices and separation is a form of racial trauma and even abuse. It asks the person who has been disproportionately affected by racism, White supremacy, and other forms of psychological and emotional trauma to forget what they have experienced and forgive the system that was designed for their failure, without correction.[11] From experience, I would say most Black people want to see if someone will stand with them in solidarity before they have an interest in racial conciliation. And whenever we lose sight of this reality, we increase the likelihood of having conversations that create more harm than good.

For churches or individuals seeking to grow in their practice of solidarity and what it means to really stand with their neighbors, it can be helpful to develop a solidarity framework for how they will practice that. I have created a solidarity framework to help people understand what it truly means to stand with people and resist oppression and injustice.

Table 2. A solidarity framework

Practical call to action	Theological understanding
Lament with others Create space for people to lament and genuinely lament with others.	The biblical text is clear that lamentation is a part of what it means to be human and journey through life with God. The New Testament contains powerful imagery of what it means to stand with people who are suffering. Romans 12 is an exhortation to believers in Rome to mourn with those who mourn. Lamenting is crying out about that which has caused injustice and suffering. This gives us an opportunity to see life from another's vantage point and stand with the laments of others. Mourning with people is ministry.
Listen to others Create healthy spaces where people can share without fear and listen to others without censorship.	There are several passages that encourage people of faith to be with people in the form of listening. In the book of James, the first chapter encourages believers to place listening above speaking and emphasizes the goodness that emerges from listening. Listening gives believers an opportunity to listen and center voices that have been silenced or minimized because of struggle.
Learn from others Take time to learn from others when you have limited perspectives.	It is important that we not only listen but also stand with people through learning. Solomon mentions the importance of wisdom in Proverbs chapter 4. He encourages readers that wisdom is essential and exhorts us to seek it. This gives us an opportunity to seek ways in which we can learn from others—there are countless books, podcasts, and documentaries that help us listen authentically.

Immerse yourself Take time to immerse yourself in the world of others.	In the book of John, chapter one reminds us that Jesus is the Word who became flesh and dwelt among people. He was fully immersed in the world around him in ways that gave others a way to think about proximity in their lives as a genuine form of the ministry of presence.
Show compassion and empathy Be aware of how others have been impacted by injustice and show compassion and empathy toward other people's suffering.	In Ephesians chapter four, the writer reminds believers to be compassionate to others, and that compassion requires humility. Compassion causes us to be with people in ways that seek to understand others' suffering, but it also gives us an invitation to stand with those who are suffering in a tangible way.
Stand alongside others Be active, engaged, and stand alongside others in the fight for justice.	A key aspect of being a part of the family of God is being concerned not only with what happens in our world but also with our neighbors and family in the faith. The book of Galatians in the sixth chapter asks us to bear one another's burdens. Injustice is not something that goes away overnight and may require struggling alongside people to carry the weight of injustice.
Use your voice Be intentional and use your voice alongside others.	Solomon encourages readers of the book of Proverbs that God is concerned with what happens to the poor and marginalized. He writes in Proverbs 31:8-9 that we should be bold in speaking up on behalf of others who are marginalized. Solidarity gives us an opportunity to lend our voices to the concerns of those who are in the fight for justice.

The practices listed in the table are all ways in which Jesus showed up in the Scriptures for those he was proximate to, and those he stood with. Jesus lamented, listened, immersed himself, had compassion for the weary, struggled alongside people in their suffering, and spoke up for those whose voices were unheard in the text. Jesus is the example of what standing with people in our world these days should look like. Jesus made clear his central focus was to be with those who were oppressed, and that calls us to be proximate in ways that enable us to stand with people. This is what solidarity work means.

JUSTICE IS NOT THE SAME AS CHARITY

This brings us to another important point of the distinction. When people think of the word *justice*, they often envision a charitable action, such as handing a man experiencing homelessness a gift card or helping someone in need. Charity like this is good, but it is very different from justice, and we must not conflate these terms. Charity is making sure that people in a food desert have access to a meal for the night, but justice is understanding why the neighborhood is a food desert in the first place. I know charity all too well because the organization that I lead attracts many people from diverse backgrounds that show up in charitable ways for those who are unhoused. But to go deeper than charity, we must ask tough questions like, What happens economically that causes one neighborhood not to be invested in while another neighborhood on another side of town does receive resources? Every year, people perform various service activities on Martin Luther King Jr. Day. But Bernice King, the daughter of MLK, has made public statements on Twitter to help folks understand that while charity is okay, justice is what we need. She writes:

> Kindness matters. But kindness is not justice. Civility counts. But calling for civility is not the humane response to injustice. Justice is. Love is essential. But love is not a passive, weeping bystander. Love puts in the work. Love implements the demands of justice.[12]

When it comes to racial division, charity and kindness are attributes. The White-led church where I served displayed this well. During my time on staff, when racial tensions emerged in our community, I was often called on to organize charitable acts of service. I was told by the pastor that we could "do kind things, but not anything to rock the boat." This struck me as odd because, as a Black man, my boat had always been rocked, tossed, and even overturned.

Still, I was not given the green light to pursue social justice opportunities to speak out about systemic issues and how they go against the character and nature of God. Whenever I spoke to the congregation, I was given assigned topics within a designated sermon series. I realized they liked the idea of having diversity on the stage as long as my voice was limited to the narrative they wanted to hear. They were proud to say we were a diverse congregation, yet they did little to become involved in the injustices that plagued our community. In the minds of many congregants, acts of charity alone were enough, and this church painted a picture of a Jesus who was only about charity. But the Jesus I learned about in historically Black churches was a Jesus who challenged the empire, flipped over tables, sat with outcasts, included women, and spoke up for the poor. Jesus was a liberator.

It was and still is my belief that real social justice involves having a compassionate heart that springs into action. The church is called to act with compassion. True compassion comprises more than good will. Christ is the greatest example of this. Because of Christ, as Galatians 3:28 tells us, "there is neither Jew nor Gentile, neither slave nor free, nor is there male and female, for you are all one in Christ Jesus." In Christ, we see the man who is the friend of sinners, one who crosses regional lines to be with people who would be considered other, and one who challenges those who held religious power and looked down on those who were less powerful. He is the one who blesses the merciful and pronounces judgment on those who oppress others.

Themes like justice and liberation are at the very heart of Black theology developed by theologian and scholar James Cone. He understood the need for a theology that allowed for understanding God through the existential realities faced by Black folks. Cone wanted to assure Black folks and scholars who spoke about God through the lens of White supremacy that God is in the midst of the struggles of Black people and that he liberates the oppressed. In essence, Cone taught that

God was and is on the side of those who are mistreated by systems of injustice.

Cone makes this bold and profound observation: "Until we can see the cross and the lynching tree together, until we can identify Christ with a 'recrucified' black body hanging from a lynching tree, there can be no genuine understanding of Christian identity in America, and no deliverance from the brutal legacy of slavery and white supremacy."[13] Therefore, understanding that justice is not charity is a revolutionary concept linked to the heart of Christ. To pursue justice is to look at what is wrong, understand the root cause, and take proper corrective steps toward change. Just as repentance calls followers of darkness to turn and walk in the light of God, justice calls us to break the chains of evil behavior and to establish that which is good.

UNDERSTANDING BEGETS SOLIDARITY

So, how do we pursue justice? This begins with solidarity and understanding. It's impossible to speak about what we do not comprehend or to reconcile a problem when we do not know its root cause. From a social justice perspective, this involves understanding how present-day behavioral patterns have been passed down from old laws that perpetuated discriminatory practices and speaking clearly to those issues. It's about learning the deeper historical implications of things and the uncomfortable process of holding up to society the mirror of self-reflection. We can only seek justice once we open our eyes and understand the injustices that currently plague our communities.

Historically, this has been a challenge. It's easy to resort to phrases like "I don't see color" as a means of inaction. But as Gregory Coles correctly notes,

When we've ignored differences in identity, people in the majority have tended to ignore the unique needs and challenges of minority identities. We think we're caring for people, with no labels—but sometimes we wind up only caring for the people who are easier to care for, the white people and rich people and able-bodied people.[14]

Seeking to understand is important because it confronts buried history and the present effects from that history. It's not cheating the process and trying to "wing our way" to doing the right thing. True social justice can be achieved only through intention and being committed to standing with people who are oppressed by systems of injustice.

Pursuing justice without intentionality is similar to attempting to assemble furniture without referencing the instructions, as I have tried. These boxes come with a set of instructions, but rather than carefully reading those instructions, I try to freehand it and piece the item together through clever guesswork. It seldom works. Halfway through my assembly process, I end up messing something up and having to examine the instructions. While they might seem like an inconvenience, they are critical to understanding what I'm attempting to put together.

When we do not understand the importance of solidarity and move straight toward justice or reconciliation, we've started to assemble something we do not understand and end up doing more harm than good. Understanding the root causes of injustice takes time, and without proper understanding, we cannot obtain clarity about how our actions could negatively impact our neighbors. It's why honoring historical background is important. Ultimately, if we love justice, we should be concerned about injustice in our communities. To love our neighbors and neighborhood is to know and understand the issues they face.

LIFE WAS MEANT TO BE PROXIMATE

In 2014, photographer Eric Pickersgill was sitting in a busy New York café when he noticed a family sitting across from him struggling to find connection and community. The father and both daughters were distracted by their phones, while the mother looked out the window with a blank stare, alone, despite being with her family.[15]

Each time Pickersgill thought there was a possibility of this family connecting and being present with each other, it was shot down by the father's announcement of something obscure he'd found online, and back to their isolated worlds they all went. Pickersgill described how each family member seemed to be in a different world and disconnected from the others, thanks to our addiction to modern technology, social media, and hyper-connectivity.

Inspired by this family's lack of connection, Pickersgill launched a series called *Removed*. This collection of photos comprised everyday people and even some of his friends doing normal activities while holding their cellphones. Then he achieved a surreal effect by asking his subjects to remain in position, took the shot, and then removed the devices in the final, Photoshopped pictures. He had one goal in mind: to reveal to the world how disconnected, busy, and isolated we have become.

There were photographs of couples lying in the same bed facing away from each other holding cellphones, children sitting next to each other but not talking to one another, parents sitting next to their children with both parents and child distracted and not connecting, and people at BBQs hanging around the grill while everyone stared at their phones. Pickersgill wanted us to realize that we need each other more than we need technology or being overloaded or busy with information. Every photo carefully drives home the important message that we miss opportunities to engage with those around us. It's not just opportunities with close friends and family members; we miss opportunities to engage with those in our communities and larger society as well, and as a result we are "removed" from the struggles and sufferings of others. We are better when we take time out to connect with our loved ones, and we are better when we stand in solidarity with those who are experiencing injustice.

This is the essence of what Mack and Rock mean when they underscore the damage done by inattentional blindness. It hurts everyone involved and goes against the teachings of Jesus, who taught that our neighbors are the people before us, the communities around us, and those we see who are suffering from injustice. Communities that do not speak up about the injustices that disadvantage our neighbors uphold oppression and grieve God's heart.

At the end of the day, we all long to be seen. To this point, several years ago I was traveling through a rural part of southern Tennessee. Confederate flags littered the area, and my sense of discomfort grew the more we traveled. Eventually, we had to pull over for gas. After parking at the pump, I went inside to pick up a few items. As I stood in line to pay, a middle-aged White couple approached. Despite my being first in line, the young White clerk acted as if I wasn't even present and proceeded to help the couple before me.

Not in the mood to create a disturbance, I remained silent. That's when another White man in the store noticed and spoke up. "Hey, this guy was here first, and you know it. You all need to grow up!" The clerk begrudgingly acknowledged me and rang up my items.

As I stepped outside, I had conflicting feelings arise within me. On one hand, I was sad. How could someone treat another human being with such dismissive behavior? But I was also thankful someone had the courage to speak up, and shortly after, the young man flagged me down and started to talk to me about the town's racist past and how they treat Black people in the town. He continued with telling me how much he has had to unlearn, what books he has read, and that he believed God cared for all. This White guy didn't know me and could have easily remained silent. But he didn't. For a brief moment, he stood with me in solidarity.

FOCUS ON JUSTICE

Reconciliation is an important theme in the Bible, and it is always part of the work God seeks to do in our lives. But before the reconciliation or conciliation can happen in the way that folks desire, we need to place a much sharper focus on justice and solidarity. Let me close with this final thought from my article in the *Christian Post* about the differences between racial justice and racial reconciliation:

> Our focus for the near future should be on racial justice, rather than skipping steps to rush to racial reconciliation. Many white Christians think that racial reconciliation solves many of the injustices that persons of color face. I think there needs to be a robust education of the differences between the two because they are not the same. Making the distinction between the two is vital because reconciliation and progress cannot organically come without first acknowledging and rectifying the historical systems that have disadvantaged black and brown people.

> While the racial reconciliation conversation is an important one to have, it cannot happen while ignoring the injustices that affect black and brown people in communities across the country. One conversation cannot happen apart from the other. Both are needed.

It is my hope and desire to see brothers and sisters walk together in the garment of destiny that MLK Jr. spoke about, and it is also my deep desire for the Church to lead this charge.

The responsibility for this lack of awareness sits with the Church. As one holding Good News, the Church must lead the conversation of both faith in a God of forgiveness and justice for God's children who are oppressed. It was James Cone [who] eloquently penned in his book, *God of the Oppressed*, "The scandal is that the gospel means liberation, that this liberation comes to the poor, and that it gives them the strength and the courage to break the conditions of servitude."

God honors all stories of creation equally, including black and brown stories that systems have oppressed. When Jesus entered the world, he did not do it for a specific group; his purpose and salvation were incorporated into each group of the world.

Jesus himself modeled what it meant to be proximate and engage in stories and conversations untraditional to a Jewish rabbi. He demonstrated this many times by taking longer routes on his way to Galilee to connect with the Samaritan woman at the well, breaking social norms to bring healing and salvation to a woman who was an outsider. Like Jesus, the Church must listen, stand in solidarity with the oppressed, go out of its way to embrace the marginalized, and take on the responsibility of educating its majority members on how to do this wholly.

The Church must be about reconciling, with justice in mind. What better way to honor God than to lean in and embrace the full stories of those who have a hue that matches the skin of Jesus.[16]

Only after we are committed to solidarity and justice can we take a hard look at some of the lies from the past and the misconceptions we harbor. Seeking justice takes us on a journey in search of the truth. And the first step along this journey is to uncover buried history and stand with those who have been unjustly treated.

APPLICATION

Have you ever had someone you didn't know stand up for you, or has it always been someone you know who has come to your defense? Or were you that person who decided to stand up for someone else when they were wrongly treated or taken advantage of? If you have ever been the person who stood up for others or had other people stand up for you, most often it is connected to a relationship. Most times we feel compelled to take a stand with people that we have gotten a chance to know, or better yet, people whose stories we have taken the time to digest and process deeply.

One way to get close to those we have never met is taking time to understand people through the lens of what has impacted them, maybe in their personal lives but also historically. It takes a person who cares to sit with, stand with, and be intentional about understanding what justice issues affect those who are different from us.

Afterward, we can understand what God says about those issues. Getting proximate enough to understand the why behind an issue can motivate us to make a commitment to stand with people whom God loves. One easy way is to start reading and learning from perspectives you have not considered before, and as you read, ask yourself some probing questions: Where did I come from? What is my story? And how does this shape how I view all of God's children? Here's a very short list of books I posted during Black History Month:[17]

- *Where Do We Go from Here?* by Martin Luther King Jr.
- *Jesus & the Disinherited* by Howard Thurman
- *The Cross and the Lynching Tree* by James Cone
- *The Souls of Black Folks* by W. E. B. Du Bois
- *Beloved* by Toni Morrison
- *Why Are All the Black Kids Sitting Together in the Cafeteria?* by Dr. Beverly Tatum
- *Go Tell It on the Mountain* by James Baldwin
- *Invisible Man* by Ralph Ellison
- *Black Man in a White Coat* by Damon Tweedy

CHAPTER FOUR

CONFRONTING BURIED HISTORY

A couple of years ago, I became friends with a brother by the name of John O. I had heard of him over the years because we have mutual friends, but when many things were opening back up from Covid, we were introduced and decided to get together for coffee. I could tell that John held similar feelings about the racial tensions surging around the country and in church communities during this time, and our conversation confirmed it. We both agreed that Black people and other people of color were exhausted and growing tired of the lack of responses from many White evangelical communities to confront structural and systemic racism in a way that held people accountable for racial acts of violence toward Black and Brown people—especially those who profess to follow Jesus.

Over coffee, I shared some personal attacks I experienced during the height of racial tension for speaking up about the murders of Black people at the hands of law enforcement, and how that stung because it came from White brothers and sisters in the faith. He shared some similar things and told me that he decided to leave the Southern Baptist Convention, a denomination he had been a part of for some time. I sat in shock as he shared about what he had witnessed and what made him walk away.

John grew up in Houston, Texas, in a Christian Nigerian household. After graduating from Dallas Theological Seminary, John served at churches in both Texas and Georgia—eventually joining the SBC. But months before our coffee, in July of 2020, John published a blog and shared in detail with his community why he could no longer remain part of this denomination. I had not heard about the blog and decided to look it up after our meeting. He anticipated some backlash for leaving, but after he posted it he actually got more support than he had expected. John's very personal and passionate blog cited four reasons for his departure from the SBC that really helps us to understand not only what ignoring buried history does but also how much courage one must have to stand for what is right in the face of those who are unwilling to lean into truth.

The first reason John gave was the destructive nature of what he called "disremembered history." John was aware of the historical racism the SBC had against Black people and people of color and noted many times the SBC struggled to speak out against racism in the past. In fact, slavery was seldom referenced. He writes, "An honest understanding of history will embrace that the SBC was really one bad marketing meeting away from being called the Confederate Baptist Convention." A second reason was the SBC's lack of desire to work at any form of racial repair that, he says, starts essentially with confronting and confession. From John's perspective, "Confession and repentance are not optional in the Christian life." Third, John pointed to the unhealthy partnerships the SBC had established with those in the Republican Party, and this alignment even included having Vice President Mike Pence speak at their annual assembly and the call from several high-profile leaders to vote for Donald Trump. The fourth and last reason was what John viewed as shallow solutions to a much deeper problem that upheld not just racism in our country but White supremacy. To him, the SBC was quick to say they wanted unity without doing the hard work of understanding the systemic racial problems in their midst.[1] All this left John to conclude, "The SBC failed people like me."[2]

There are so many ways I can empathize with John's perspective, but I couldn't imagine how much strength he and his family had to have to take a stand like that in a public way. John's convictions about confronting buried history pushed him to take a stand for what he felt was right and what he felt honored God and the children of God that were being overlooked because of this "disremembered history." No matter whom you align yourself with, you have to admit walking away takes courage. His stance and blog communicated that it was no longer acceptable to bury history and refuse to confront the major systemic flaws that exist in many of our churches and society. Years later, John has recently stepped down as a pastor to rest and focus on his communal business and school. He is still doing well and also still speaking and preaching—just in a different way. I'll never forget him telling me how much healthier he felt after his decision to leave the SBC. It's overwhelming to think about how much the year 2020 revealed and the many things that were swept under a rug.

HOW 2020 CREATED A SHIFT

Entering the fall of 2020, I'd hoped the pain I felt inside would subside and that after the presidential election, life would return to normal. But this was not to be. The Christmas season of 2020 was difficult. At the same time as many of my White friends celebrated Advent, I also noticed this growing trend of other White people I knew speaking out on social media in full support of the presidential election protests that were going to take place on January 6. This made little sense to me. While many of these same Christians were willing to celebrate the life of an infant who came to earth in humility, they also seemed willing to join in on what will go down in history as the insurrection to support someone who was not humble at all. How could some of the people I had known, who volunteered with the organization I lead, and who had conversations with me and my family over meals, ignore the racial trauma that was tearing apart our nation and support a president who stoked the flames of White supremacy? How could people be upset with me for speaking up about the murdering of a Black man (for which the murderers were later convicted), but then support someone who boldly made racist remarks during his presidency? Moreover, how could people show up in workspaces, worship in church with BIPOC, and deny them the right to speak about how it all affected them? As I sat in my living room and watched the events of January 6 unfold, I felt sick to my stomach.

The same fear I had experienced after George Floyd's murder resurfaced, and I found myself struggling to breathe. Each new image that appeared on the screen felt like yet another hand clamping down on my neck, offering an additional squeeze. I think much of Black America felt Floyd's words "I can't breathe" a little more. The images of pro-Trump protesters knocking down barriers, breaking windows, and waving Confederate flags, and of police officers being sprayed with mace, were gut-wrenching. The sight of people who fell off walls and lost their lives defending a man who was so divisive was beyond my comprehension. Then came reports of the individual who had been shot to death inside the Capitol. These images took me back to conversations I had had with my grandfather about the struggles he had gone through. I worried, wondering to myself, *Will history repeat itself?*

That day redefined many of the relationships in my life. Individuals I once counted as allies and well-meaning people now stood against everything I knew to be true. A few people I once considered friends took their families to the Capitol that day. One of them was quite belligerent on his social media posts and said that he was teaching his children about "real history." Concerned by this messaging, a mutual friend of ours gave him a call and asked if he realized what he was doing and the pain he was causing people like me and his other Black friends. Rather than listen, this brother cursed and hung up. It all seemed to be slipping away, as Covid-19 continued to expose where Americans stood in terms of racial relationships.

Looking at the "Make America Great Again" signs that littered the Capitol that day, I could only think to myself, *Make America great for whom?* For most of America's history, America was not great if you had my skin color, and according to my grandfather, he had never seen it nor experienced it when he was my age. MAGA had become both a symbol of racism and something that emboldened White supremacists to come out of their hidden places to speak up.

WHICH HISTORY DID YOU LEARN?

Sometimes White leaders talk as though there are two separate histories in America. This is especially true when it comes to books and documentaries about the country's founding years. Stories about America's might, economic prosperity, and ascension to greatness abound. Much has been written about 1776, the economic rise of the nineteenth century, the emergence of the United States as a superpower during World War II, and how America has led the way in innovation. But in these films and books, White individuals are always the centerpiece. It is essentially a whitewashed history.

When it comes to Black America, few prominent faces have graced our history books, especially in the books I used in high school. Black history is always talked about in terms of slavery and trauma rather than from the perspective of its inclusion in the collective history. It is as though there are two Americas: one Black and one White. But the truth is that Black history is a part of US history. Although painful, it is a part of our shared history.

This is a point that criminal defense attorney Jeffery Robinson came to realize. For years, Robinson served as a lawyer but had little understanding of how askew the criminal justice system really was. But one day, Robinson found himself caring for his thirteen-year-old nephew, and he had an awakening that he would have to tell him about racism in America. This meant he would be forced to learn about history and share experiences with him from his upbringing. It set him on a path that would eventually lead him to unpack the history many have attempted to avoid. In the process, he became an advocate for criminal and racial justice reform. He could no longer be silent.

Today, he speaks around the country, frequently to White audiences, doing his part to uncover those parts of our history that have been suppressed. I love his passion as a teacher and agree with him when he states that while the racial scars of our past are not our fault, they are part of our shared history.[3] Only when looking closer at our history can we discover the parts we have missed. In a recent interview with the *Portland Mercury* while premiering his documentary *Who We Are: A Chronicle of Racism in America*, Robinson said, "One of the most important things, right now, is reclaiming our history. A history that has been stolen from all of us. The most ominous conversation about this is sparked by the George Orwell quote. 'He who controls the past controls the future. He who controls the present controls the past.'[4] Robinson is speaking about not only reclaiming buried history but confronting the ugly truths about history that we sometimes run from.

EXPOSING THE LIES OF THE PAST

Talking about the history of race relations in America means we must be willing to take a hard look at our past and honestly evaluate our shared history, our whole history. In *Lies My Teacher Told Me*, James Loewen details how our history books have marginalized systemic injustices, elevating individuals who accomplished much but held few moral values. Unfortunately, lies about the history of Black people in America started being told the moment the first twenty slaves landed in Jamestown in 1619, and they continue to be propagated to this day.

To this point, I feel like every day I continue to unpack parts of my buried past I never understood. My grandfather continues to share stories from his childhood and upbringing and the history of our ancestors before enslavement that blows my mind each time I get a chance to listen. At the same time, older Black volunteers that serve with our organization share their experiences with racism. Each time I am confronted with one of these new realities I realize there is so much buried history that goes beyond the enslavement of Black people in this country. There are times when I want to share with some of my White friends that Black history did not start with slavery. To start there is to miss a huge opportunity to understand the worth that our ancestors carried long before they were enslaved. In his first official address as housing and urban development secretary under President Trump, Dr. Ben

Carson reflected on the founding of America and made this faulty observation:

> That's what America is about. A land of dreams and op-
> portunity. There were other immigrants who came here
> in the bottom of slave ships, worked even longer, even
> harder for less. But they, too, had a dream that one day
> their sons, daughters, grandsons, granddaughters, great-
> grandsons, great-granddaughters might pursue pros-
> perity and happiness in this land.[5]

These words make little sense to me. Black people were not immigrants. They came in the bottom of slave ships under the most brutal conditions, and a visit to the National Museum of African American History and Culture would inform any person of this, even those like Carson who forgot about his blackness. For hundreds of years, Black children were doomed to a life of slavery, regardless of whether their father was White and had raped a Black woman. In South Carolina, Black people were whipped and executed for growing their own food or as-sembling in groups. And then there is the uncomfortable re-ality that forty of the fifty-six signers of the Declaration of Independence owned slaves.

Even our national anthem contains these words in its third verse: "No refuge could save the hireling and slave from the terror of flight or the gloom of the grave." While space limita-tions preclude a full analysis of this verse, it's clear that this was not an anthem written with people of my color in mind, and yet many wonder why so many Black athletes have a dif-ficult time rising to celebrate this song. It was written by Francis Scott Key, who thought Africans should be property. In the article "Where's the Debate on Francis Scott Key's Slave-Holding Legacy?" published by the *Smithsonian* magazine, Christopher Wilson, the director of experience design for the

National Museum of American History, documents these important truths about Francis Scott Key:

> In 1814, Key was a slaveholding lawyer from an old Maryland plantation family, who thanks to a system of human bondage had grown rich and powerful.
>
> When he wrote the poem that would, in 1931, become the national anthem and proclaim our nation "the land of the free," like Jefferson, Key not only profited from slaves, he harbored racist conceptions of American citizenship and human potential. Africans in America, he said, were: "a distinct and inferior race of people, which all experience proves to be the greatest evil that afflicts a community."[6]

With very little scholarly research, one can find many credible sources on Key's involvement with slavery. Key literally fought for people to keep Africans enslaved. Sadly, it wasn't until I was in my late twenties that I began to understand some of the deep misconceptions that I, a Black man, carried about the history of Black people in this nation. But once I uncovered one lie, it was as if Pandora's box had popped open: I began to see the many ways Black history had been buried. It helped me gain an even greater appreciation for people like Colin Kaepernick, who kneeled during the national anthem not out of hatred for America but out of deep mourning that the very words in this anthem were not written with individuals like him in mind and instead composed by someone who fought for slavery.

Take Juneteenth, for example. As Tisby notes in *The Color of Compromise*, Juneteenth "remembers the day in 1865 when slaves in Texas finally learned about their emancipation. It is the oldest-known celebration of Black freedom from slavery."[7] Until my late twenties, I had no idea this was the case.

Part of my response to learning about Juneteenth was embarrassment. But this soon turned to anger. How could I attend a public high school for four years, go through college, and not recall a single mention of this historic event? Because it was not taught. It is also symbolic of those who were enslaved in Galveston, Texas, who did not experience freedom until almost three years after it was proclaimed. Juneteenth reminds us that we must no longer allow freedom to be delayed. On June 19, 1865, enslaved Africans in Galveston heard General Order No 3, proclaiming their freedom. The news they received was of liberation, but it was also ironic because the Emancipation Proclamation was signed on September 22, 1862. It took all that time for the enslaved Africans to have their individual freedoms publicly affirmed. What's more ironic is that in the same way their freedom was delayed, knowledge about that event has also been delayed for many people in our country. It has taken 155 years for this information to become public knowledge. While Juneteenth has been recently recognized as a federal holiday, voter suppression remains, and the erasure of Black history and the true liberation and freedom of persons of color in many ways remain delayed. The more I uncovered, the more I realized large segments of Black history were entirely missing from my understanding. This made me weep.

For many today, the main issue of the Civil War was states' rights, not slavery. Hence, many believe that men like Robert E. Lee and Jefferson Davis, though wrong in their thinking, were men of valor. But the Civil War was not about a disagreement on public policy, and neither was it a replay of the War of 1812. It was, simply put, about slavery, and any attempt to make it something else continues to bury its true history. That's why it still stings when Blacks see Confederate flags flying proudly. To us, it means the person flying it wants to go back to a time when Black people were property. That's why the insurrection was so triggering as Confederate flags took the Capitol. We must move past the chatter of today's public pundits and read the actual words that a Southern leader such as Confederate Vice President Alexander H. Stephens wrote in his 1861 "Cornerstone Speech." His speech is documented on websites such as The American Battlefield Trust, which archives historical Confederate artifacts to remember conflicts that happened on the battlefield, as stated on their site. In Stephens's own words in Savannah, Georgia,

> Our new government is founded upon exactly the opposite idea; its foundations are laid, its corner-stone rests, upon the great truth that the negro is not equal to the white man; that slavery subordination to the superior race is his natural and normal condition. This, our new government, is the first, in the history of the world, based upon this great physical, philosophical, and moral truth. This truth has been slow in the process of its development, like all other truths in the various departments of science. It has been so even amongst us. Many who hear me, perhaps, can recollect well, that this truth was not generally admitted, even within their day."[8]

Even Abraham Lincoln issued these words in a documented address that he gave on August 14, 1862, as cited by the University of Michigan in their collected works on Abraham Lincoln from 1809 to 1865:

> You and we are different races. We have between us a broader difference than exists between almost any other two races. Whether it is right or wrong I need not discuss, but this physical difference is a great disadvantage to us both, as I think your race suffer very greatly, many of them by living among us, while ours suffer from your presence.

In a word we suffer on each side. If this is admitted, it affords a reason at least why we should be separated.[9]

This is America's true and whole history. There is no possible way to be a committed antiracist if we aren't willing to grapple with the ways history impacts our present. Like Jeffery Robinson, I believe there are two Americas portrayed. One is whitewashed and pristine and one has impacted countless Black people and people of color in horrific ways even to this day. But sometimes I ask myself what my living grandfather or Black people and Indigenous people who are still fighting for reparations would say. I agree with Robinson when he states that there is a dual nature to America. That in one breath there are many great things that happen here, but it doesn't mean that the foundation on which this country is built is not a harmful one. Robinson says it this way: "You can be a great country and be a country built on White Supremacy."[10] These two things can be true. We can have a nation of promise and opportunity today while still carrying the deep scars from our past, scars that continue to divide us.

One of these prominent scars was Jim Crow and the discrimination from it still carried in the hearts of those who abhor racism.

RECONSTRUCTION, JIM CROW, AND CIVIL RIGHTS

My wife's grandfather, John Henry, grew up in Augusta, Georgia, as a country guy who loved being outdoors, fishing, and working on his truck. Whenever I'm around people who lived during the era of segregation, I feel compelled to ask them about their experiences because something special happens when we pause long enough to see life through the lenses and experiences of others. Also, I love learning how history has shaped my family in ways I was not there to see, because in many ways this history continues to shape me. John Henry shared stories about growing up in the final years of Jim Crow and school segregation, not drinking out of the same water fountains as White people, and riding in the back of the bus. My grandfather's stories are the same stories John Henry had, but he also told me about certain parts of the city he could not visit as a Black teenager. I couldn't imagine not being able to visit certain parts of town or the country because of my skin—while on second thought, there are still parts of this country that I would not want to visit because of the ingrained racism. Stories like these make me think of Sandra Bland, Tamir Rice, and Trayvon Martin.

To understand my own grandfather's history, we must go back to just after the Civil War during the Reconstruction era. This period was an attempt to bring the country together, address the major challenges slavery had caused, and offer a clear path forward for former slaves to integrate into society. Thankfully, there was some progress. As Michelle Alexander notes, "In 1867, at the dawn of the Reconstruction era, no black man held political office in the South, yet three years later, at least 15 percent of all Southern elected officials were black."[11]

But this would not last, and soon everything grew worse. In his heart-wrenching work *The Cross and the Lynching Tree*, Cone writes, "Lynching as primarily mob violence and torture directed against Blacks began to increase after the Civil War and the end of slavery, when the 1867 Congress passed the Reconstruction Act granting Black men the franchise and citizenship rights of participation in the affairs of government."[12] Those in the South were furious with the advantages that were now being afforded to Black individuals and feared they might lose control. On this point, Michelle Alexander writes, "The backlash against the gains of African Americans in the Reconstruction era was swift and severe. As African Americans obtained political power and began the long march toward greater social and economic equality, whites reacted with panic and outrage."[13]

For a few years, the North's influence on the South effected change. But as Union troops began to pull back, a new era of Black oppression began, prompting Isabel Wilkerson to write, "The law went nominally out of effect during the decade known as Reconstruction, when the North took control of the former Confederacy, but it returned in spirit and custom after the North retreated and the former enslavers took power again, ready to avenge their defeat in the Civil War."[14]

This new era was known as Jim Crow, and it sought to erase any advances Black people made during Reconstruction. Jim Crow laws instituted by southern Democrats remained in effect until 1965. These restrictions included racial segregation in public facilities, limited opportunities for Black children, and a reduction in voting privileges for Black adults. Tisby states, "Jim Crow proved devastating for Black people. White racial terrorism during Jim Crow resulted in horrific atrocities like the development of the convict-lease system, reproducing what is often called 'slavery by another name.'"[15]

Jim Crow made it infinitely easier to institute discriminatory laws such as redlining (i.e., withholding services from potential customers in neighborhoods deemed hazardous to invest in, usually at the expense of minority communities). Within months of Blacks beginning to flourish in the South, becoming politicians and leaders in communities, and working together with White leaders, segregation laws rose that sought to deepen the divide between Whites and Blacks.

While some are quick to point out to me that we live in different times today, I always offer some pushback. Yes, times are different, but the undercurrent of racism persists. As Austin Channing Brown notes:

We don't want to acknowledge that just as Black people who experienced Jim Crow are still alive, so are the White people who vehemently protected it—who drew red lines around Black neighborhoods and divested them of support given to average White citizens. We ignore that White people still avoid Black neighborhoods, still don't want their kids going to predominantly Black schools, still don't want to destroy segregation.[16]

Seeing racial division as an opportunity to win influence in the South, Republican leaders in the '50s and '60s extended olive branches to many White supremacists. This became known as the Southern Strategy, and it featured political leaders such as Richard Nixon and Barry Goldwater. Frank Brown documents this explicitly in his research, "Nixon's 'Southern Strategy' and Forces against Brown." Brown indicated,

Despite the wishes of the Reconstruction U.S. Congress, the U.S. Supreme Court changed and in 1896 the Court, in *Plessy v. Ferguson*, upheld a Louisiana statute requiring "separate but equal" facilities as meeting the Equal Protection Clause of the 14th Amendment. Louisiana outlawed integrated rail travel within the state. In the 1954 Court, *Brown* (1954) reversed the decision in *Plessy v. Ferguson* (1896) and held that the state-enforced "separate but equal" doctrine was in violation of the equal protection clause of the 14th Amendment.

The executive branch of government represented by the President of the United States gets involved in public education when it is to his political advantage; and that is what President Richard M. Nixon did in 1968 when he sought the Republican nomination for president. *Brown* gave birth to the modem reform movement via public vouchers and other educational reform measures under his "Southern Strategy" that was designed to gain the votes of individuals who opposed school desegregation and the votes of northern Whites who did not wish for their children to attend school with urban minorities, but who did not have the resources to move to White isolated suburban communities.[17]

This is important to note because the "Southern Strategy" became a prevailing mentality in the South and in the hearts of many White people. This strategy also sought to advance the narrative of White supremacist groups such as the KKK, leaving MLK Jr. to remark:

> The daily life of the Negro is still lived in the basement of the Great Society. He is still at the bottom despite the few who have penetrated to slightly higher levels. Even where the door has been forced partially open, mobility for the Negro is still sharply restricted. There is often no bottom at which to start, and when there is, there is almost always no room at the top.[18]

While many try to point to King and the civil rights movement as the end of racism in America, the truth is that many White Americans during that time simply became better at concealing their racist ideologies. The move was from de jure discrimination to de facto discrimination. Today, overt racism is scorned, but subtle racism is still accepted in many communal and institutional settings because it's a disposition, it is institutional, and in many ways it is structural. Many say they hate racism but continue to embrace racist habits fueled by the old ways of our racialized society. Eddie S. Glaude Jr. is correct when he states, "Racial habits are formed by the outcomes we see in the world rather than by the complex processes that produced those outcomes."[19] In other words, we look at statistics that show discrepancies in the criminal justice system or Black employment and form racial biases instead of confronting the systems that created the problem.

So what do we do? How can we break this ongoing, apparently endless cycle of moments of racial reckoning followed by years of silence? The answer is this: We must break the silence and break free from the lies we hold dear to our hearts that cover and bury the truth about our whole history by confronting it. We must break our harmful routines.

BREAK THE ROUTINE

Several years ago, I settled into a poor routine. For too long, I had sacrificed everything I had to build a nonprofit organization. This was an especially stressful season. For the first three and a half years, I couldn't even take a salary and served as a full-time volunteer, often working sixty to seventy hours a week. Unfortunately, food became my primary coping mechanism to manage stress. Every meeting and interaction I had seemed to revolve around it. When I was in my office, I ate. When I came home, I ate. When I was out working with volunteers or staff, I ate. Food became my Goliath, and it was soon apparent I was losing the battle.

It all came to a head when I visited my doctor, and he let me know that if things did not change soon, something bad could happen. That exchange spooked me, and I left her office resolved to do something different. Normally, when faced with a stressful conversation, I would pick up a bag of Doritos and get to work. But that day I had little appetite. Instead, I headed straight to a local gym, purchased a monthly membership, and got to work.

To be honest, my first few workouts were brutal and quite discouraging. I lost my breath quickly. But little by little, I substituted my food addiction with better alternatives. I ate healthier, worked out consistently, learned about how food and calories worked, and within five months had lost fifty pounds. Nothing about my new routine was easy, but I was willing to confront my challenge, accept some accountability from others, and embrace a new way of living.

I use this example because racism is a public health crisis. And just as improper nutrition can damage a body, harboring racial biases can destroy a soul and damage the body of Christ. Breaking this routine can be difficult, but it is possible.

Several years ago, I was invited on a podcast to talk about one of my books. The host was a White male named John who wanted to educate his audience about race relations. However, as the interview continued, it became obvious to me that this host's routine revolved around a schedule that only placed him in proximity to people who were just like him, namely, White. As is often the case, sometimes people who are trying to be about the work don't live the work themselves.

John asked me what White people could do to build communities with people different from him, and if I am honest, I paused long and hard before I responded with an answer to the question. When I responded, I challenged him to think about the normal rhythms in his life and asked him to share his schedule of things he did throughout the week. John began to list the places he frequented. These included White coffee shops, White hangouts, and White sections of town. And soon, he understood why I asked him this question in response to his own. He started to realize that he was asking a question, but he had not broken his own routine of not being proximate to the very BIPOC communities he had me on the podcast to advocate for. I pushed back by pointing out that each place he listed was in direct contrast to the people he said he wanted to be in relationship with. I challenged him to start incorporating some spaces in his routine that would break up the comfort of always being around people who were like him, such as visiting a Black-owned coffee shop and entering with the openness to sit at someone else's table.

A few weeks later, John contacted me, rather excited. He had started incorporating new routines and before long had met a Black gentleman in his midseventies and established a relationship with him. This man began to share his history, and even offered parenting advice to my young White friend, who learned all about what it meant to be a great father and husband. This new relationship only happened because John was willing to break with his routine, and it allowed him to learn about Black history from a living, breathing person who experienced that history firsthand.

This is also what Jesus did when he came to earth: he met people where they were, even if he had to break up his routine to do so.

APPLICATION

Placing yourself in the shoes of my friend who invited me on his podcast, ask yourself a few of these questions:

- What do your weekly routines look like?
- Do they include places that people of color frequent?
- Are you often in contact with children of God who look different from you?
- Do you gravitate toward monoethnic or multiethnic settings?
- Do you only frequent businesses that are owned by majority culture, or have you been intentional about supporting BIPOC businesses?

If your response to these questions parallels my friend John's, I would encourage you to step out of your comfort zone and shift your routines. Start attending church services that are not predominately one ethnicity. Visit restaurants that feature a diverse group of guests. Organize your kids' recreational times so that they associate with children who look different from them. I am often reminded of Jesus in how he would break his routine and wander in parts of town that were not his own, meeting people a Jewish man had no business associating with by law. But Jesus did it anyway because Jesus came to earth to be proximate with humanity. Living in proximity with others is life changing not only for the recipient but also for the giver. When we give of ourselves to be proximate with others, something within us changes. Break your routine.

UNPACKING BIASES

In March 2019, I prepared to lead a ribbon-cutting ceremony for the launch of our Dignity Museum. I, alongside a team of people, launched the first museum in the United States that represented home-lessness, and guess what? It was out of a shipping container. My reason for doing this was twofold. First, I wanted to create a space that would center the voices of those who were overlooked, allowing them to share their own struggles and triumphs, and to debunk false ideas that might be held against this community. Second, I wanted to create a space that provided narrative justice for this community in an approach that edu-cated people in a healthy way about this subject. Through interactive technology, re-search, storytelling, exhibits, and thought-provoking questions, the Dignity Museum challenges visitors to confront their ideas of homelessness and what it takes to escape it. I started this new initiative to share the stories of the forgotten while presenting the unjust causes for the disparity in resource allocation. This includes stories of those born into poverty, those who became unhoused as adults, the kids holding cardboard signs at stoplights begging for money, and their collective fight to beat their circumstances. The Dignity Museum is designed to take the guest through a journey to promote a hopeful future of equality, opportunity, and justice.[1] The goal of doing so was to address the biases against and stereotypes of people experiencing homelessness.

From my experience, people unfamiliar with unhoused communities tend to carry a set of beliefs that inhibit their ability to understand the challenges these communities face. I wanted to create an immersive experience that would cause people to reflect on and confront these myths. It was my own way of inviting people to confront their biases by helping them learn about the strong connection between race and class. Additionally, I knew that getting people together from all walks of life in a space where they could pause long enough to engage with information they would otherwise not have would increase the opportunity for them to have more empathy toward the unhoused community.

Several hundred people came out to this grand kick-off. This was a golden opportunity to educate them on the differences and strong connections between race and class. We gave away numerous dignity awards, including one to human rights activist Elizabeth Omilami (daughter of civil rights leader Hosea Williams). But perhaps the most impactful moment was when we gave an award to one of our community members named George. As someone who experienced homelessness for several years, George did not the fit the stereotypical mold. He had a business degree, read multiple books a week, and used to be in corporate America. But when tough times hit, he found himself on the streets for over seven years, unsure what to do next. After he came to Love Beyond Walls, we walked with him until he got back on his feet and made the transition out of home-lessness. This involved getting him an updated ID card, a stable job, and his own place to stay. It took over a year before he was able to maintain a steady job and return to some semblance of the man he was before.

It was an incredible journey, and we asked him to come back for our grand opening of this new initiative to share his story. As he shared with the crowd, he spoke of the harsh encounters he faced whenever he walked into a coffee shop. People took one look at this man with tattered clothes and ragged hair in front of them and came up with a whole set of misconceptions. Sometimes when he stepped into public places such as the laundromat, people would call the police or shoo him away. Even though he often had money to pay for his needs, shop owners harassed him and made him feel like a second-class citizen. People clapped at his points, made the "hmmm" sounds in agreement, and even cheered as he spoke.

But that morning as he stood well dressed on the stage for the launch of the Dignity Museum, he said something that will always stick with me. After sharing his story and addressing the excitement around the launch of this new museum, he took a moment to reflect, saying, "Today, you see me as someone who has my act together. I'm well dressed, articulate, and have a full-time job. But the truth is I'm still the same person today I was when I was experiencing homelessness."

I've thought about that statement many times since then. George's worth as a person did not increase when he cut his hair, showered, and put on a suit. It was other people's percep-tions that had changed. People's biases caused them to mistake him for someone they did not trust, someone they thought was a threat. This is something we do all the time. We tend to as-sociate worth and value with external appearance. But in doing so, we forsake the essence of what a person possesses inside.

Afterward, a White lady pulled me aside and said that as George spoke she felt convicted and realized how she, through her entrenched biases, had contributed to the invisibility of the unhoused community. She had not grown up in a diverse community and generally thought Black people suffered with systemic poverty because of choices they had made. Only as she interacted with Black people caught in a cycle of poverty did she began to make the connection between the two in her mind. As she spoke, I admired her courage and honesty, and it challenged me to be bolder in speaking up on matters of injustice, such as racial discrimination.

UNCONSCIOUS BIASES

Bias is part of being a broken human being. It is a way of seeing, it is a heart transfer, and it is a set of intangible values that can be passed down knowingly or unknowingly. When I mention bias here, I am talking about those biases that keep us from being with each other, understanding one another, and standing with people in solidarity like all God's children should. Sadly, bias serves as a magnet to those who want to maintain a single narrative and are content to harbor prejudices and favor one group of people above another. "Everyone in the world has some kind of cultural bias," Anthony Casey writes, "either toward the good of their own culture or negatively toward another culture."[2] But as Casey continues, "The key is not to pretend you have no bias, but rather to identify your biases ahead of time."[3]

While many people like to think racial bias is a thing of the past, the truth is many have just become better at disguising their racial discrimination. Black feminist author Patricia Hill Collins writes:

Racism didn't magically go away just because we refuse to talk about it. Rather, overt racial language is replaced by covert racial euphemisms that reference the same phenomena—talk of "niggers" and "ghettos" becomes replaced by phrases such as "urban," "welfare mothers," and "street crime." Everyone knows what these terms mean, and if they don't, they quickly figure it out.[4]

Biases can easily be handed down from generation to generation without much thought. And before we go any further, we need to examine different types of bias. The first of these is *explicit bias*. This form of prejudice makes no qualms about asserting one group of people above another. It's the bias Black leaders like me have faced when we're viewed as aberrations just because we can lead, speak, and sound articulate. Explicit bias involves holding a set of assumptions about a group of people and refusing to allow new information to challenge your viewpoint. It's saying, "This is how the world is and there is nothing others can do to shift my perspective." White individuals who hold this belief often look at a topic such as diversity and immediately jump to questions to explain away the need for diversity. The preconceived bias they hold prevents them from looking at this topic from any other angle. They have this embedded belief that anything that uncovers history is a threat to their whiteness or existence.

Next is *implicit bias*, which is often unintentional and comes out in ignorant phrases people say. For example, I can't tell you how many times White people have looked at my 6′2″, 270-pound frame and said, "You must play basketball." They have no desire to stereotype, but they merely state what they observe in front of them. They see a middle-aged, tall, healthy Black male and make their assumptions.

Another form of bias most people don't think about is *attentional bias*, which is "the tendency to prioritize the processing of certain types of stimuli over others."[5] I've seen this play out in many forms. For example, there have been times I've been walking to a Christian conference with a group of fellow believers. Our intention is to enter a building and worship Jesus. But as we walk and come across marginalized, unhoused, and often Black individuals, I see these very people on their way to worship a God who made everyone in his image look the other way and ignore those around them. Homelessness and interacting with people who look different from them felt uncomfortable, and their brains immediately triggered them to ignore the unfamiliar and look the other way.

Confirmation bias is yet another form to address. This tends to lend itself to those people who don't want to hear any other perspective than the one they have in their minds. They prefer a single-story narrative, as Chimamanda Ngozi Adichie described in her TED talk. Born into a conventional middle-class Nigerian family, Adichie recalled her family having servants that she regarded as inferior. But she was surprised one day when she visited her servant boy's home and discovered one of his siblings had made a beautiful patterned basket. This startled her because it had never occurred to her that members of this family were capable of making anything. Adichie shares how all she had heard about this family was that they were so poor, and this made it impossible for her to see them as anything but this. Eventually, after Adichie moved to America, she experienced the reverse form of confirmation bias. American roommates at her university had a preconceived perspective of people who came from African nations and didn't believe she could perform simple tasks like cooking on a stove. They were also shocked to learn that English is the official language of Nigeria. As she shares, single-story narratives are highly problematic: "Show a people as only one thing, over and over again, and that is what they become."[6]

This brings us to *affinity bias*. This form causes us to gravitate toward groups who are like us and to steer clear of others who are different. Instead of branching out and making new friends, we frequent the same stores, restaurants, and social settings as people who think and act like us.

Each of these five biases works the same way in matters of race by keeping us from getting to know those who are different from us and reducing them to a caricature. Instead of holding a negative view of someone because they have less than us or are otherwise different from us, we must do the more humane act of getting to know that person, affirming their dignity rather than stripping it away with bias.

Biases take many forms, and it is critical that we surround ourselves with others who call out and challenge us to think through the misconceptions we hold. During the Supreme Court nomination process for Justice Ketanji Brown Jackson, I watched as some tried to disparage and diminish her, associate her with critical race theory, often unveiling their own racial bias in the process. But then I watched Senator Cory Booker offer a heartfelt statement that brought Jackson to tears. Looking into her eyes, he made this observation:

> I'm telling you right now, I'm not letting anybody in the Senate steal my joy. . . . We appreciate something that we get that a lot of my colleagues don't. And I want to tell you that when I look at you this is why I get emotional. . . . You are a person that is so much more than your race and gender. You are a Christian. You are a mom, you are an intellect, you love books, but for me, I'm sorry it's hard for me not to look at you and see my mom, not to see my cousins—one of them who had to come here and sit behind you. She had to have your back. I see my ancestors and yours.[7]

Bias is everywhere. It's something we've all experienced to some degree. But it is critical that when these biases emerge, we are people who speak up and speak the truth.

IT'S TOUGH FOR MAJORITY CULTURE TO SEE BIAS

During my time working at a historically Black church in the heart of Atlanta called Wheat Street Baptist Church, I served as the social justice and witnessing pastor under Dr. Ralph Watkins.

I always appreciated Ralph's perspective and engagement in the community. Every day, I saw him step outside his church office and interact with people on the street, many of whom were experiencing homelessness. He would listen to them, invite them to church, and hear their story. Furthermore, Ralph was intentional about incorporating a language of embrace into his Sunday sermons. There was this notion about being for and in the whole community, which included our neighbors without an address.

As I grew to know him, I realized Ralph's response went back to his days under the late William Homes Borders. During the civil rights era, Pastor Borders became an outspoken leader in the Black community, and when he wasn't giving his own sermons, it wasn't uncommon for MLK Jr. to venture down to Borders's church and listen to him speak. As Ralph shared with me, Borders had this practice of making his office the front porch of his house. This allowed him to engage with his community. Day after day, Borders would walk the local neighborhood and engage with Black residents and hear their stories of injustice. Ralph ended up adopting these same practices long before he knew he would become pastor of that church.

Ralph's response was common among many Black Christians I observed in this Black church tradition of engaging those who are impoverished and live on the streets. The majority of Black people in the United States have a deep understanding of poverty and oppression, either through personal experience or close family connections. I have engaged those who had relatives who lived during the Tulsa Massacre and have engaged those who know what it's like to be oppressed to the point that entire communities were placed in jeopardy. Thus, there is empathy for those who share the struggle. I know this is my story. My years of working with those experiencing homelessness forever changed my view of people and the world. And there is a certain level of empathy we develop when we have been proximate to the margins of society or knowing people who have gone through challenging times.

Contrast Ralph's response with many White Christians I have encountered. Often, when I would speak at a White church on the subject of homelessness, a White congregant would pull me aside and say something like, "I'd like to help, but I'm afraid. I don't know what to do." I realized the basic problem was that many White people had never experienced life with people who were unhoused. One person even told me, "I have never spoken to a Black man experiencing homelessness." As a result, they harbored internal biases.

One day in particular helped me to understand the depth of this challenge. I was in charge of hosting an outreach somewhat like a health fair at Wheat Street Baptist Church that would allow us to bring people in off the street and offer basic medical services, including check vitals, foot care, and a hot meal. The theme of our day was "Gather Atlanta," and my goal was to bring together as many different groups as I could to serve the community. Represented in this sea of faces were Blacks, Latinos, Asians, and Whites. Our goal was to extend the Lord's Table to our community so it could experience the love of Christ.

As this event continued, a White family walked up to me. The mom was in tears and said, "I just want to thank you all."

"Why?" I replied.

She explained how this get-together had been a complete eye-opener. Never before had she imagined hearing the stories she was listening to from those experiencing homelessness. It destroyed the false bias she had. No longer could she believe homelessness was limited to drug addicts and those who refused to work. She saw with her own eyes and encountered everyday people who were just like her, people who had suffered a lot in life and had no one to walk with them. Seeing this changed everything for her.

This interaction reminded me of a few realities. First, it's hard to see the real hurts of others if you do not live in geographical proximity to them. Also, if you socialize only with people who are just like you, it is difficult to understand the pain of others outside your circle.

IT'S ALL ABOUT THE HEART

Some mistakenly think of bias strictly in legal terms. But this leads us to the difference between de jure and de facto discrimination. *De jure* refers to matters of law. For example, slavery was the law of the land in America and other Western nations. It gave White people the legal authority to discriminate and act on their racial biases against others, and historically we've seen this play out in laws that literally keep Black people from voting, buying land, marrying certain people, attending schools, and a number of documented laws related to the Jim Crow era. Jim Crow at its core was about laws that not only segregated Black people from White people, but laws that also maintained a level of power and social order over Black people that strengthened the racial divide.

However, after those laws were changed and the de jure restrictions were lifted, the de facto practices of racial bias remained. Just because Black people were allowed to sit on any seat of a bus they chose and just because separate water fountains were removed, it didn't mean these biases stopped.

For those who approach the conversation of race from a legal perspective, conversations such as we're having in this book might be confusing and lead them to ask something like, "Wasn't racism eradicated from America during the civil rights era?" And from a de jure perspective, they have a point. Black people today have far more legal rights than their ancestors.

But from a de facto point of view, racial bias continues to color many decisions that are made related to the criminal justice system, housing, education, and government funding. Part of dismantling these biases involves understanding how such history has warped our views of one another.

This comparison points us back to Jesus' Sermon on the Mount in Matthew 5–6. Jesus preached this to the religious leaders of his day, who felt that because they were not murdering others or sleeping around with women who were not their wives, they were good people and worthy of eternal life. But Jesus challenged these assertions and took their understanding of God's commands a step further. He showed them that the reason God gave the instructions he had in the Old Testament was to speak to the condition of the human heart. Consider these two passages from Matthew 5:

> You have heard that it was said to the people long ago, "You shall not murder, and anyone who murders will be subject to judgment." But I tell you that anyone who is angry with a brother or sister will be subject to judgment. (vv. 21-22)

> You have heard that it was said, "You shall not commit adultery." But I tell you that anyone who looks at a woman lustfully has already committed adultery with her in his heart. (vv. 27-28)

Rule keepers despised him because his standard of justice was more personal and got to the heart of the matter. Matthew 15 is another pivotal example. Jesus is talking about the importance of honoring one's parents. In the context of this passage, Jesus was addressing individuals who were fulfilling the legal obligations to take care of their parents, but they were not honoring their parents. God had commanded adult children to care for their mothers and fathers in their old age, but religious leaders had stepped in and given family descendants another option. They could take those same funds they might have given to their parents and give them to the temple instead. The twofold result was the religious leaders grew richer while adult children appeared more virtuous and could speak of the ways they were "giving to God." All the while, parents suffered and were dishonored.

This understanding prompted Jesus to quote from Isaiah 29:13 and say, "These people honor me with their lips, but their hearts are far from me" (Matthew 15:8). As the late Christian philosopher Dallas Willard wrote, "What is in our 'heart' matters more than anything else for who we become and what becomes of us."[8] The list of heart examples we could take from Jesus' ministry is endless, but think about this interaction he had with the rich young ruler in Mark 10:

> As Jesus started on his way, a man ran up to him and fell on his knees before him. "Good teacher," he asked, "what must I do to inherit eternal life?"
>
> "Why do you call me good?" Jesus answered. "No one is good—except God alone. You know the commandments: 'You shall not murder, you shall not commit adultery, you shall not steal, you shall not give false testimony, you shall not defraud, honor your father and mother.'"

"Teacher," he declared, "all these I have kept since I was a boy."

Jesus looked at him and loved him. "One thing you lack," he said. "Go, sell everything you have and give to the poor, and you will have treasure in heaven. Then come, follow me."

At this the man's face fell. He went away sad, because he had great wealth.

Jesus looked around and said to his disciples, "How hard it is for the rich to enter the kingdom of God!" (vv. 17-23)

Notice how this ruler makes the case a lawyer might make. "I'm a good person because I keep all the rules." But Jesus' response reveals the ruler's lack of commitment. He was okay with fulfilling Jewish custom, but he was not all right with giving all he had to follow Christ.

It's all about the heart. It's about being aware, acknowledging the pain, and acting.

TEARING DOWN BIASES

When it comes to dealing with racial biases, we need to go through our own teardown process. For example, there are some things from history we should be willing to confront and remove. One example of this is the killing of George Floyd, which sparked a racial awakening and widespread protests around the country that reignited efforts to remove Confederate and other statues viewed as symbols of White supremacy, slavery, and racism.

Why, you might ask? A national report by the Southern Poverty Center found that there were almost 1,700 monuments that represented the Confederacy in public spaces.[9] These hundreds of symbols uphold this type of racial violence and hatred toward Black people and other groups that have been harmed by White supremacy. There was obvious backlash coming from people who said those statues were a part of history and had nothing to do with slavery, but again, those narratives held a one-sided story that, honestly, I struggle to understand as even a point of discussion. What civil society would want to commemorate individuals who raped, enslaved, and were responsible for genocide against an entire group of people?

I remember reading a story on September 8, 2021, when residents in Richmond, Virginia, gathered and began to chant, "Whose streets? Our streets," and "Na na, na na na na, hey hey hey, goodbye," in response to the removal of a large statue of Robert E. Lee.[10] To those present, this was not only a historic moment but also a personal one because, in the eyes of many, Robert E. Lee represented White supremacy. He was brutal to those who were enslaved, and his statue was a symbol of that hatred.

His statue coming down involved an entire community of people from different backgrounds coming together to denounce what was evil and commit to a better way, saying this is a part of history that we must confront and grow from as a community. It was a moment of solidarity to say this type of deconstruction is necessary, and it was important for children from all different backgrounds to see this moment. The *Harvard Gazette* spoke to legal scholar and professor at Harvard Law School Annette Gordon-Reed about the pulling down of statues and what it represented. They asked her, "What do you say to those who argue that the removal of such statues in prominent public settings dishonors the memory of those who died fighting for the Confederacy?" Her response was powerful:

> I would say there are other places for that—on battlefields and cemeteries. The Confederates lost the war, the

rebellion. The victors, the thousands of soldiers—black and white—in the armed forces of the United States, died to protect this country. I think it dishonors them to celebrate the men who killed them and tried to kill off the American nation. The United States was far from perfect, but the values of the Confederacy, open and unrepentant white supremacy and total disregard for the humanity of black people, to the extent they still exist, have produced tragedy and discord. There is no path to a peaceful and prosperous country without challenging and rejecting that as a basis for our society.[11]

When my White friends wonder why these types of Confederate statues need to be removed, I ask, "What if your family, ancestors, and people from your community were raped, stolen, sold, beaten, left for dead, and oppressed? Would you want a statue of one of the people who contributed to that in your front yard?" The answer would probably be a solid no.

This is what I mean by deconstructing. It is the removal of things that uphold White supremacy and represent the heart and mentality of racism, even if that mentality is embedded in harmful theologies that seek to dehumanize those who are vulnerable. That is a stand we all can take. It is looking at the "disremembered history" that John O. spoke about and saying "enough of this" because every child of God matters. But we must realize that taking this type of stance will cost something. It will cost standing with people who may be different yet need to be affirmed in a way that screams they are God's children too. It means challenging theology that holds up all forms of racial hatred so people can experience the liberating love of God. As my friend Robert Monson said in a recent Twitter post, "Being an 'ally' to Black people must transcend the latest news cycle. I think often of the fervor of people in

2020 to come to our rescue, throw a few dollars, read that one book on not being fragile, and Black out squares. . . . Did those things continue? Fatigue set in for many. . . . Liberation is costly."[12]

This type of deconstructing leaves behind it room for people's hearts to be renovated in a way that is healthy. The vast majority of White Christians I encounter would agree in principle that racism is wrong. This is a starting point that previous generations have not shared. We are all created equal in the image of God, but we must be real in understanding that has not always been on display, and there are still statues of the heart upholding this ideology that need to be torn down. Deconstruction is about confronting the parts of history that need to be understood and being willing to release and get rid of everything that remains that is influenced by White supremacy. Why? So you can truly have a heart for the neighbor God has called you to love. A part of loving God is standing in solidarity with others who might not be experiencing that love because things block the way for them to say, "I am God's child too."

What embedded biases would you confront today if God asked you to take a look within? Be willing to challenge them, tear them down, or do whatever it takes to remove that which might be keeping you from loving your neighbor fully.

APPLICATION

First Corinthians 12:24-26 says, "But God has put the body together, giving greater honor to the parts that lacked it, so that there should be no division in the body, but that its parts should have equal concern for each other. If one part suffers, every part suffers with it; if one part is honored, every part rejoices with it."

Confronting biases starts with internal interrogation and the willingness to be honest and wrestle with ideas we might have dismissed as false. It also means understanding that solidarity in-volves standing with some while standing against anything that has the power to rip us apart. And it involves rooting out and deconstructing any biases keeping one child of God from being part of the body with another Christian.

What are some ways you have experienced bias and witnessed biases against others? When others suffer from bias, do you suf-fer with them? Are you willing to lean into the pain your brothers and sisters of color experience when their communities face in-justice and hardship? Every part of the body matters because every part represents a child of God's creation.

ENGAGING DIFFERENCES

The other day I was in an important meeting when I received an urgent text from my daughter. "Dad. Dad. Dad," she texted, avoiding the usual "hey" greeting. I knew something was up, so I quickly responded.

"Zion, what's going on?"

"Dad, I was on the way to class and the vice principal stopped me. I was wearing my African scarf and she said I had to take it off because it was a hat. When I tried to explain it was a scarf that was part of my culture, she said 'Well, most people only wear these hats for religious reasons, such as Muslims.' I told her I wasn't Muslim,[1] but that this was part of my heritage."

After I read this follow-up text, I responded with the question I hate asking my kids: "Was she White?"

"Yes," she replied, inserting a tear emoji with her response. Not the somewhat sarcastic emoji, but one I could tell expressed genuine hurt.

I responded that I would be with her shortly. After wrapping up my meeting, I drove across the city to her school and had a conversation with the vice principal because I understood something that this principal did not: when Black youth develop racial identity, it is very fragile. I affirmed my daughter's words and explained the meaning and significance of head wraps. I shared how this was trending in the world of fashion and that the practice of head wraps dated back to the precolonial history in Africa and that they marked the status of marriage and family.

I explained how during the transatlantic slave trade, head wraps were one of the few items enslaved individuals were allowed to bring. But shortly after African women arrived and were viewed as property, head wraps became a symbol of oppression. White slave owners used these same head wraps to identify which women were enslaved and to whom they belonged. While this cultural symbol came from Africa, it became a tool of White supremacy during enslavement. It was disgusting that I had to even teach my daughter this lesson while she was thirteen and trying to embrace her racial identity, but now I needed to educate her White vice principal as well.

Fortunately, the head wrap being a symbol of oppression has begun to change some as Black women have reclaimed the head wrap and have made it a part of asserting proud blackness. According to Eman Bare, "In recent years, the natural hair movement has begun to reclaim these garments and the fashion industry is taking note. Head wraps even appeared at New York Fashion Week with models walking down the runway in afro-centric wraps and garments. But these pieces are more than a trend, and they still hold deeply-rooted symbolism for many African-Americans."[2]

I informed the vice principal that in recent years, Black women have embraced such things as the natural hair movement, whereby they celebrate their identity and heritage.[3] The result has been a resurgence in Black women who do not conform their hair styles to match that of White culture and who allow their hair to grow out naturally. Part of this movement involves things such as head wraps and embracing blackness in a way that has not been celebrated well in US history.

I drove to my daughter's school because this topic was important to me. As the father of Black children, I've struggled with the many complexities that come with raising kids in a racially divided society and always find it hard to give the Talk in many ways. I hated to see my daughter's racial identity challenged and wanted her to be proud of her heritage and the skin that she is in.

To the vice principal's credit, she listened and wanted to hear what I had to say, and she humbly admitted her ignorance and lack of understanding. Afterward, she called Zion into her office, apologized, affirmed her identity, and assured her it was okay to wear her head wrap, and most important, it was okay to be who God made her to be. My daughter was relieved, and this turned out to be a valuable teaching and healing moment. Why was this moment so important to me? Because I didn't have that type of advocacy growing up to help me value my blackness.

However, as I left the school and drove to my next engagement, I thought about all the times this happens every day in society, not just to Black people, but to people of all racial backgrounds. I thought of Asian Americans who face racial discrimination and who grieve for the people who were killed in Atlanta by the spa murderer or who were being violently attacked for no reason at all in neighborhoods for simply walking down the street.[4] My heart went out to Hispanic Americans who face many stereotypes that threaten to hold them back, including being seen as only valuable for working in privileged neighborhoods. I had seen the mistake this vice principal made replicated in numerous churches that lacked crosscultural competency and how lives of BIPOC people are, in fact, shaped by history. As a result, many individuals, such as my daughter, experience hurt.

EXCLUSION CAN BE DESTRUCTIVE

In light of the recent policies aimed at excluding those without homes from doing everyday activities, I found myself connecting power to all exclusions that BIPOC groups face. Power plays a significant role in the distribution of resources in society.

A key example of this is the Chinese Exclusionary Act, which systematically excluded Chinese persons here in the United States. According to *The Chinese Exclusion Act*, a PBS documentary, the "1882 law . . . made it illegal for Chinese workers to come to America and for Chinese nationals already here ever to become U.S. citizens."[5] And as this documentary revealed, it was those who held power to write and pass laws that excluded groups like Chinese workers while framing narratives about groups who are targeted by policy.

Exclusion is common in American society, and it's something we have all experienced to some degree. A friend of my family who is a Black woman on an all-White staff at a church tells of the microaggressions she experiences and the hurtful things she has had to endure from people who say they follow Jesus. She shared with us that she cries three to four times a week at church. There is the continual fear that if one does not fit in with the crowd, one will not be accepted.

Think back to those times in your life when you suffered exclusion. Maybe you remember what it was like to go out for PE and be one of the last ones selected for a sports activity. Perhaps there was a time in your twenties when you discovered after the fact that a group of your friends went out for an exciting night on the town, but you were not invited. When you began your career, remember how it felt to show up at your office for the first time and feel like an outsider. Or maybe as you grew older in age, you found your grown children seemed to push you out of their lives. These painful experiences are microcosms of what African American men and women feel every single day.

Sometimes exclusion is vicious and intentional. I know this from personal experiences. Figure 1 is a well-known chart that we adapted and use at the Dignity Museum that illustrates differences between exclusion and real inclusion.[6]

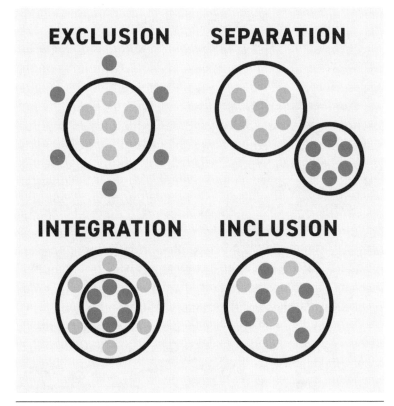

Figure 1. Differences between exclusion and real inclusion

Sometimes Black people are excluded in a vitriolic manner. Examples of this include redlining, stop and frisk, and the war on drugs, which targeted Black and Brown people. But a more common example today is separation. It's cities using major interstate highways to divide their populace between White and Black. It's programs designed to create separation between different ethnic communities, it's White supremacy that uses power to define and even silence the worth and voices of those who have been overlooked and oppressed by systems of injustice. Integration honestly isn't any better, because it often involves exclusion within an institution or community. It is often being accepted only with lines drawn around you. The underlying message is often "We will allow you to integrate, so long as you follow the rules of majority culture and remain in your place."

This reminds me of the story of six-year-old Ruby Bridges, who, on November 14, 1960, became the first Black child to attend an all-White school, William Frantz Elementary. The response from the crowds of people who stood in protest is gut-wrenching to watch, as is listening to White people telling her she didn't belong there. This same thing continues to happen in many places but in quieter ways. Integration sometimes is stopping short of fully including people and creating a place for them to fully belong.

June 14, 2020, offers one such example. It was a Sunday morning during the height of the Covid pandemic and of racial injustice protests across the country. Author and pastor Louie Giglio invited Dan Cathy and Black hip-hop artist Lecrae to talk about race in response to the George Floyd and Breonna Taylor shootings. The goal was to inform Giglio's congregation, predominantly White and middle class, about racial injustice.

The conversation started out fine, with Giglio asking Lecrae several questions about race to educate his congregation.

However, it took another turn altogether when Giglio mentioned he did not want to use the term "White privilege" when discussing racial injustice because he thought the term was too offensive for those in his congregation. He suggested Lecrae use the phrase "White blessing" instead, to help his predominantly White congregants better engage in the race conversation. Giglio said slavery was a "White blessing" because it benefited White people.

Not only did Giglio co-opt a term used to describe systemic and structural racism, but he also revealed just how fragile and privileged he was by changing a word to be more accepted by his White congregants. His use of "White blessing" dismissed four hundred years of enslavement, structural racism, Jim Crow, mass incarceration, and many of the injustices faced by a person of color in this country to this day. In her piece in the *Washington Post*, Sarah Bailey reported the following:

> The 70-minute conversation between Giglio, Lecrae and Chick-fil-A's CEO Dan Cathy at Giglio's Passion City Church in Atlanta was supposed to bring an awareness to racial inequity in America to Giglio's majority white evangelical congregation and followers. "We understand the curse that was slavery, white people do," Giglio said. "And we say that was bad. But we miss the blessing of slavery, that it actually built up the framework for the world that white people live in."[7]

The backlash from Giglio's exchange was powerful. The next day, someone shared a video recording of the conversation on Twitter, which ignited many antiracist activists because a notable White pastor had called Black suffering a "White blessing" to a Black man, while trying to make the race conversation more palatable to his White congregants. I remember seeing that whole thing online and the responses of trauma that Black people and people of color experienced for the lack of belonging created.

I have seen variations of this conversation play out in countless settings.

DIFFERENCES CHALLENGE OUR PRECONCEIVED BELIEFS

Dr. Cornel West, distinguished scholar, professor, and writer, observed, "The aim of a constitutional democracy is to safeguard the rights of the minority and avoid the tyranny of the majority."[8] Unfortunately, this objective is often not achieved as racial prejudices tear us apart.

But when it comes right down to it, race is a social construct that distracts us from God's original intent. We are all members of the human race, but many of us have used race as a tool of oppression and, greater than that, a form of violence that harms people and claims their lives. As Michael Emerson notes, rewards tend to be unequally allocated to each racial group. "Race matters profoundly for differences in life experiences, life opportunities, and social relationships."[9] We must be very clear about this, making it as real as it was for my daughter to experience what she did in school from that principal. No, the amount of melanin in one's body doesn't make one person better than another at all, but because sinful humans have decided that race is an indicator of worth, a White person cannot help but look different from someone who is Black.

To this point, Beverly Daniel Tatum makes an interesting observation: "I am asked, 'Can people of color be racist?' I reply, 'The answer depends on your definition of racism.' If one defines racism as racial prejudice, the answer is yes. People of color can and do have racial prejudices. However, if one defines racism as a system of advantage based on race, the answer is no."[10] We live in a racialized society, and in the words of MLK Jr., "Racism is a philosophy based on a contempt for life. It is the arrogant assertion that one race is the center of value and object of devotion, before which other races must kneel in submission."[11] Again, sometimes this happens overtly, and sometimes it is subtle.

While I was pastoring at that predominately White congregation from 2015 through 2018, I was behind the stage one Sunday helping the lead pastor prepare for a sermon. As I did so, he turned to me and asked, "How would a Black person say this?"

I wasn't completely surprised with this form of subtle microaggression. It was the type of thing I often experienced while serving in predominately White institutions. In many of these communities I felt seen, but in this instance, I felt ignored. This is what we call epistemic injustice. It is injustice in which people are seen but not heard.

In their article "Seen but Not Heard," published in *Lancet*, Havi Carel and Gita Györffy use Miranda Fricker's work to explain what epistemic injustice is and how it affects people. They document that Fricker saw that epistemic injustice happens in two forms and is a type of injustice that happens to the knower. Carel and Györffy write:

> [Fricker] identifies two such wrongs: testimonial injustice and hermeneutical injustice. Testimonial injustice occurs when prejudice causes a hearer to unfairly assign a lower level of credibility to a speaker's testimony or report. This can be done by doubting, ignoring, or failing to take someone's testimony seriously until it is corroborated by another. For example, a person who is biased against people of a particular race or gender may unfairly assign lower credibility to testimonies given by speakers from those groups. Another kind of epistemic injustice is hermeneutical injustice, which occurs when a gap in

collective interpretative resources puts a speaker at a disadvantage. This injustice occurs when society as a whole
lacks an interpretative framework to understand particular experiences.[12]

The question from the lead pastor was a prime example of
the inattentional blindness present in many of these spaces. It
was a complete failure to understand, or care to understand,
the differences between our two cultures, and how this would
be harmful to a person of color, given that slave masters used
to put enslaved ministers up to speak only to limit and control
what they would preach about to make sure the other persons
who were enslaved would have the fear of God not to disobey
their master. It was triggering.

While I'm sure I didn't fully hide the shock on my face, I did
my best to answer respectfully with something like, "I would
just speak from my heart and let God guide the rest."

Dissatisfied, he read a line from his notes and asked the
question again, as if I needed an example to make me understand. "So, would you just move your hands around like this?"
He did his best "Black preacher" mime.

I excused myself and reiterated my earlier reply that he
should "depend on the Spirit of God to direct him in whatever
way the Spirit chose."

The entire experience felt like a microaggression, and I
would later learn from those on staff that the head pastor felt
threatened by me and my ability to express myself passionately. People responded well to my sermons, and he felt the
need to single me out, perhaps to make me feel self-conscious.
I know that his motivations may not have been entirely based
on race: he was likely acting out of fear, worried he would lose
control of his congregation and concerned that their love
would turn in another direction.

While my skin color may not have been the sole motivating influence, it is worth noting that of the many pastors on staff, I was the only one who drew such a response from the pastor. No one else was questioned in this way. He never asked any of my colleagues, "How would a millennial pastor read this?" or "How would a former drug-abusing pastor read this?" Neither do I believe he looked at me and said, "Now, there's a Black preacher. I think I'll single him out based on his race and make him feel uncomfortable." He simply did not see me for who I was because he did not understand my story.

This is exactly why learning the history of others and engaging with cultural differences is crucial. Our actions are so often instinctual, and we unknowingly form habits based on our homogeneous pasts. Confronting our buried history helps us realize all God's children are important and helps us stand with those who are oppressed.

"AREN'T YOU THE JANITOR?"

Consider another example. I was a keynote speaker at a predominately White Christian event. I arrived wearing my book bag, and as I entered the sanctuary, the greeters stopped me with looks of confusion and concern. "Are you sure you're in the right place?" one said.

"I'm pretty sure I am," I replied with a smile.

Even though I knew what was going on, I've found I can usually defuse such situations with a little kindness. I rattled off the name of the event, to which they nodded and hesitantly let me inside. I took a seat in the back and watched as the host introduced the session and, eventually, me, prompting the crowd's applause. As I walked toward the stage, the greeter from the door, who by now suspected I was a security threat, rushed after me down the aisle, yelling, "Sir? Sir!"

He had almost caught up to me when the host pointed and said, "Oh, and here's Terence now!"

That experience was a mixture of humor and sadness. I still chuckle when I think of the expression on the exasperated greeter's face, but I'm also pained by the unintentional blindness directed against people of my color and how it often prevents some White Christians from loving their neighbors as themselves. Did I mention that I was there to give a talk on compassion? That hurt deeply.

Antonio Gramsci, author of *Prison Notebooks*, is known for his theory of cultural hegemony, which addresses the way people tend to run together and how ruling classes use cultural institutions to maintain power in capitalist societies. These sorts of power structures can become deeply embedded in monolithic thinking, and I would argue that this type of hegemony has crept its way into the church. As a result, these embedded beliefs prevent us from engaging with differences and uncovering our buried history. If you hold power, you also get to choose who is deserving and who is not.

I'm reminded of these embedded ideals whenever I grow my hair out, walk into a store, and am mistaken for the janitor. The image of a Black man with natural hair being the leader of a nonprofit organization does not compute for many White individuals.

Toward the end of 2021, I was selected by a well-known real estate foundation as one of four leaders representing nonprofit organizations to be in the running for a three-year, 100K grant to help bolster Love Beyond Walls. I pulled up to the building and had those usual pre-talk nerves before I spoke, which is something I appreciate because I think they keep me grounded. I walked into the room and noticed that the board I was about to present to was all White.

I was wearing a black dress coat and white dress shirt. One of the White women on the board walked up and greeted me. She asked, "Oh, are you one of the people who is going to speak on behalf of the organization?" It almost came off that she was looking for a White presenter, and the only reason it came off that way is because of the smirk she gave immediately afterward as if she were disappointed I was not visually to her standards.

I responded, "Well, no. I'm the one who is going to present."

She responded with a "hmm," and a brief smirk flashed across her face. It was clear she did not think I could deliver. For the next forty-five minutes, as I delivered my presentation, I was met with a sea of disingenuous stares and received numerous questions that were not asked of the other three White presenters who came before and after me. I had to insert credibility points, such as my enrollment in a graduate program, to prove myself and ease their concerns. It was awful, and it left me to question myself. Was my appearance or hair wrong for the occasion?

After I left the room, I was so emotionally drained that I went out to my car and wept. *I know I'm not crazy*, I kept saying to myself. *I know what I just experienced.* Later that week, I took to Twitter to share my thoughts and posted my experience. To my surprise, I received hundreds of comments from Black individuals saying they had experienced something similar. I had been gaslit and shamed into thinking less of myself.

I followed this up with a tweet to my followers that resonated with so many people:

Dear Grantors,

Black and Brown nonprofit leaders are not charity cases. We are intelligent carriers of dreams that have the power to create social change and disrupt the status quo and injustice that oppresses communities of color.

We are multi-faceted, multi-talented, and well-rounded commu-nicators. We are brilliant innovators that have learned to create without a table. Respect us as such and stop questioning our profes-sionalism because we are different from what you are used to funding.

Even if someone is different and does not meet our cultural ideals, we have no right to shame them, or allow a racialized society to dictate how we show up to love our neighbors. We need to create belonging in the spaces that claim to be welcoming of all. Differ-ences are an invitation to learn and break down barriers that divide.

ASSIMILATION, INCLUSION, AND BELONGING

I've often spoken on the importance of topics such as assimi-lation, inclusion, and belonging related to both my anti-poverty and antiracism work. In the words of Helen Turnbull, "Assimilation is defined as the need to adjust our style to fit within the dominant organizational and/or cultural norms."[13] Assimilation embraces someone else's way of doing something. It asks a Black person to set aside who they are to be something they are not. I have experienced this many times in many White spaces—all informed by race. It's putting on a school or work uniform to conform to a set of standards and feeling at church like we are challenged to be something totally different and not our whole selves.

Inclusion is a bit different. It's letting someone know they can be a part of the group, but they are not free to live out their full uniqueness as a person. As Sydnee Crews, a DEI manager, writer, and workshop facilitator asks, "If one must assimilate to be accepted, is that really inclusion?"[14] Understanding this through the lens of racial bias is particularly important. Not only are Black people asked to assimilate, they are asked to do so under the weight of racial bias. This is more than just so-cially conforming; it's asking a person to literally forget who they are in order to be accepted. This is what we might refer to as "limited inclusion." It's saying, we will accept you, but with the condition that you operate like the majority culture.

In 2019, I was asked to speak at Georgia Tech University to a group of aspiring architects to infuse more empathy for those experiencing homelessness as the architects considered making design decisions. My talk revolved around the phrase "hostile architecture." This is an urban-design strategy that seeks to construct environments that make it more difficult for the unhoused population to remain in that community. This might include bolts on steps, large boulders in areas where unhoused individuals might cast a tent, fencing under outside stairs to limit shelter, or handrails between bus stop seats to prevent unhoused individuals from lying down. There was even a case in West Palm Beach, Florida, where the children's song "Baby Shark" was played on loop to annoy and discourage individuals experiencing homelessness from remaining in the community overnight.[15]

Hostile architecture is an aggressive attack on the unhoused community and a reminder of the lengths to which people will go to distance themselves from others and say, "You do not belong here." The more I've thought about it, the more I've noticed a connection between hostile architecture and having a hostile disposition toward someone who has a different color of skin. Yes, we have largely eliminated physical barriers that create racial division, but we continue to permit invisible ones to remain. Black and Brown communities face ongoing issues with lack of quality grocery stories, health care, and quality job opportunities. The physical barriers are gone, but the invisible barriers remain. And these invisible barriers make it difficult for Black individuals to truly belong and stand in solidarity with the neighbors God calls us to love.

Everyone, whether the richest person in the state or the unhoused individual at the street corner, wants to belong. I would argue that belonging is the ability to create a safe space where people feel like they are able to be a part of community without giving up parts of their selves to be received by that community. Belonging is when people find healthy spaces where their full selves are affirmed without pretense. Creating space and engaging differences say you belong here and are free to take up space.

ENGAGEMENT HAPPENS AS WE NOTICE PEOPLE

When we erect invisible barriers, we push others away and convey to them that they are harmful and we want to hold them at arm's length. But Ephesians 2:14 tells us Jesus broke down the "dividing wall of hostility." That is who Jesus is. Jesus is the direct antithesis of hostile architecture and hostile mistreatment. Instead of holding himself at a distance from contagious lepers, Jesus was proximate. Rather than protecting his reputation by not speaking with a prostitute, Jesus spoke to her with genuine love. Instead of giving in to the popular demands of religious leaders and seeking the path of power and prestige, Jesus was a friend of outsiders. And rather than continue Jewish tradition and avoid the region of Samaria, Jesus journeyed right through its heart and even made one of its citizens the focal point of a parable.

Jesus engaged. He was gentle with people and affirmed their identity as being a part of the family of God. When I look at the life of Jesus, I see a transformational figure who offered salvation and provided a model for the most fulfilling way to live. Race and nationality were not issues because Jesus saw who people were and offered all of them the same opportunity to believe and follow him.

Engagement starts with noticing people. Instead of looking through them or staring at the floor, we look into their eyes and see them as God's creation. When I encounter someone who looks different from me or emerges from a different social location than me, especially people experiencing homelessness or racial discrimination, I like to ask them basic questions such as, "How is your day going?" This creates an opportunity for them to share. I've always been fascinated by people and enjoy sitting with them, not to interrogate them but to learn where they are in their lives, to get to know people truly to build friendships and relationships. It's not about treating people as projects; it's simply about forging new friendships with others who are a bit different from us. Some people make conversation complex, others want to dominate the conversation, and still others wait until their interlocutor is finished talking to provide a rebuttal. Yet what is often missing in these manipulative exchanges is real engagement.

A few months ago, I headed to a meeting at a coffee shop. As I approached, I saw a fellow standing outside. It was cold, and I walked right by him. However, I immediately felt bad because I hadn't acknowledged him, and I noticed other people doing the same. I realize how much of an injustice being unnoticed is to someone without an address. Backtracking, I left the buddy I was scheduled to meet and walked back to my new friend and began a conversation. He mentioned that I was the first person to talk with him, and I asked him how his day was going. He shared how he had lost his job, was living on the streets with his family, was a hard worker, and would do anything to provide for his family. In other words, he was hoping that someone would see him. "What do you need most right now?" I asked him.

He gestured toward the coffee shop and said, "A cup of coffee. They wouldn't let me in because I'm dirty and living on the streets."

This angered me, and I motioned for him to join me. We walked into the store together, and as we did, people's heads whipped around. Even the baristas behind the counter bowed their heads, quick to cast judgment before hearing the full story.

I share this because breaking down racial barriers is difficult. It challenges our embedded theology and ideals and pushes us to engage with people for who they are—namely, individuals created in the image of Christ.

Therefore, we must be willing to engage differently than we are accustomed to while remembering it should not be at the expense of placing ourselves in places that would be harmful. I want to be explicitly clear that I am not advocating for naive proximity that accepts harm, discrimination, or sacrifices people on the altar of shame. I am advocating that people use wisdom when entering into spaces to discern if a space is safe or not—especially for BIPOC persons. I know this all too well, but even to this day the pain I have experienced has not kept me from building crosscultural relationships with people and crossing those lines like Jesus did. I encourage you to cross those lines too.

Be like Jesus and resist systems that continue oppression. Be willing to speak like Jesus spoke, engage as he engaged, and share the good news to the poor as Jesus shared.

APPLICATION

Everyone has cultural blind spots. If you think you don't, I would challenge you to think back to where you were ten years ago and consider the ways you have changed your perspectives on issues in the past. How do you think differently from a decade ago? What public policies would you support or not support? How do you speak differently? How do you live differently?

The key to addressing blind spots is to surround ourselves with people who can challenge our embedded ideals or who represent something different from what we may have held onto that wasn't even true. After all, it's hard to stand with other children of God in solidarity if secretly we are comfortable with being separated from them. This week, make an effort to have a conversation with someone who might think differently from you about something that has affected them politically or even racially. Allow your listening to bring you closer to their story and to challenge your viewpoint and sharpen what you believe. This is a great way of removing blinders that can sometimes cover our eyes and keep us from being with people without having bias noise playing in the background of our thoughts.

ENGAGE YOUR COMMUNITY

Whenever we engage community, it must be done with love, not walls. This idea is reminiscent of a time I was driving from Atlanta to Washington, DC, with some buddies when we stopped in a small town in South Carolina. I was in the middle of a campaign for Love Beyond Walls, where I decided to walk across the country to bring attention to poverty and racial division, and decided to stop to use the restroom. It was a White neighborhood, and I looked for one of the main gas station chains that might have a public service area, with no success. The closest thing I could find was a couple locally owned gas stations that doubled as community service stations, the kind where you could fill up your car, get an oil change, and order a pizza all in one stop. The only thing they didn't have were restrooms.

Feeling a bit desperate at this point, we drove down the street another couple of blocks, and I came across this church with several cars parked outside. It wasn't a

Sunday, but some event was taking place as people streamed in and out the front doors. Wanting to be polite, I walked up to the front doors and knocked. A White lady opened the door, and when she saw me, she did a double-take and ensured the door only remained open a few inches as she asked what I wanted.

When I asked if I could use the restroom, she looked me up and down, and turned to a White gentleman behind her. He threw up his hands, shook his head no. She turned to me and said, "I'm sorry. We can't help you."

I stood stunned in disbelief. Seconds later, I walked back the few feet to my car and rejoined my friends Ali and Johnny, still in shock over what I had just witnessed. This woman didn't know me from Adam and had no idea I was in the middle of a campaign to stand for people who were looked down on by society. But from a quick scan of my figure and the color of my skin, she deduced that I was not someone she could trust to allow in the building. It didn't matter that we worshiped the same Savior. To her, I was a Black stranger, and I couldn't be allowed in. Moments later as I was walking away, I noticed them letting two other White men into the same church. I was heartbroken.

A few minutes later, I found a public restroom, and we were on our way. But as I sat in the car and thought about this encounter, I wept. I felt the discrimination and shame. The irony of that moment is that this church likely told stories of ways Jesus had helped those who were marginalized. Their kids' Sunday school programs likely included the story of the Good Samaritan, Jesus telling little kids to come to him, the encounter Jesus had with the woman at the well, and many other times Jesus stood for the oppressed. But when I showed up, looking different from someone they were used to seeing inside the four walls of their church, I was rejected.

Thankfully, that's not the end of the story. After returning to my car, I and my buddies traveled down the road several miles. There, I knocked on the doors of another church and was met with a very different response. Another White lady answered the door, but this time she welcomed me with open arms and even called the pastor to come meet me. As we spoke, I shared the story of what had just happened. Immediately, he issued me and my friends an apology and confessed that a spirit of racism hovered over churches in the community. And a few minutes later, he took me and my buddies out for lunch.

Two churches, but two very different responses. One engaged with walls and the other engaged with love.

These examples illustrate how easy it can be to say we love Jesus and still reject those in our communities he has called us to value. Often, before we engage our communities the way Jesus would want us to, we must strip away forms of discrimination and the personal biases that hold us back and get to know people's stories and even their historical shaping. How can we love people if we are not open to standing with people around us?

I don't have all the answers. But I do know community immersion always starts with a posture of humility. Proximity isn't only about being physically close to someone. It also includes a mental, emotional, intellectual, and spiritual connection. It's connecting with the same types of people Jesus connected with and doing all in our power to serve them with the heart of Christ.

CRAFT YOUR OWN VISION

When it comes to engaging our communities, it's easy to latch on to something someone else is doing and make their vision our own. We read a great book or watch a helpful documentary and decide we want to copy someone else's vision. But the truth is that God has granted each of us with unique gifts to stand with others in our communities.

Engaging communities that are not our own is not just about awareness; it's about reaching out and being present and understanding what's going on in your heart. The vision of how this is done emerges from your heart and is usually connected to how you spend time, what you consume (read and listen to), and who you are around.

My philosophy has always been to engage communities with a palms-down philosophy and look for ways to serve. Palms up says "give me," whereas palms down looks for ways to love our neighbors, see others as our neighbors, and look at them not as projects but as people deserving of relationships.

I love the story of Lazarus in the Bible. After Jesus received word that Lazarus had died, Jesus went to Lazarus's sisters, Mary and Martha, and comforted them. We know the ending to this story: Lazarus is raised from the dead. But before this ever occurred, he engaged those who were hurting.

While theologians have wondered for years as to the true source of those two words in John 11:35, "Jesus wept," it seems apparent that Jesus' grief was genuine. This weeping was a part of holy lament. It was a part of standing in solidarity with those who had been affected by trauma. Jesus didn't just cry for the sins of the world; he cried because he felt and experienced the pain of personal loss and saw the grief experienced by others he loved. His was a natural human response to a human tragedy. Jesus was so close to his friends, his neighbors, that when one of them suffered, he suffered. What if the way that we confronted history moved us to immerse ourselves in the world of another, stand with another, and proclaim that we are all God's children?

This is the way I want to live. If someone I love is in pain, I want to share in their sorrow. And if one of my neighbors experiences joy, I want to share in their excitement. Several years ago, my mom remarried, and I've had the privilege of getting to know my stepfather, DeWitt Walker. As we have talked, I learned what a fascinating history he has. He was one of the pioneers who helped schools to integrate in Augusta, Georgia. He was an active member of the civil rights movement, knew what it was like to face discrimination, and did what he could to stand for justice in the face of difficult odds. As I understood his story, my heart better resonated with his. When I heard about the ways he had been hurt, I hurt. And when I saw the ways this prompted him to become an activist, I was challenged to do more.

Unfortunately, things like racial biases, poor ideologies, unchecked political allegiances, deceptive news and media commentators, fear, jealousy, and envy all become barriers that keep us from getting to know others. But the greatest way to break down these barriers is through total proximity of mind, body, and spirit and being willing to be with people without making them projects. By *projects*, I am referring to when people are inauthentic in their approach to standing with other people—stripping people of their humanity by making them an achievement to brag about or a checklist item instead of fully getting to know a person, building a deep relationship with them, or even understanding their full humanity and history. We see this so much in church under the guise of surface-level discipleship making.

In no way am I saying that proximity is the one solution to the entire racial problem in our country, but I want to be clear that we have been in a wilderness in regard to race. I understand historically that proximity alone has proven not to address the deep issues pertaining to race, but I also know that racial issues cannot be solved by being apart. I believe that's why strong allies take opportunities to stand in solidarity with groups that have been oppressed by systems of injustice. Both structural change and proximate relationships are needed for people to truly stand in solidarity with all God's children. As Christians, we have a faith built of service like Jesus, and proximity is taking on the heart of a servant. But service is not one-sided. It is mutually beneficial. It's a concept rooted in the book of Acts when people sold their possessions to care for one another and broke bread together.

PLACE YOURSELF IN UNCOMFORTABLE POSITIONS

When it comes to serving others, the posture of the heart is everything. We do not serve as mini saviors. It's not about us and what we can do. It's about offering help and hope to others with the right motivation. Doing this can be hard. Some neighborhoods have different narratives that undergird their communities, either individually or collectively.

I think of a Black friend of mine who pastors a multiracial church in a White community. Trump signs are everywhere still long after his time in office has come to an end, and in some respects, he is very out of sorts with his community because this community hasn't really embraced him. Still, he sees this place as the place he is supposed to do ministry for now. He has shed tears on the phone with me over the discrimination that he has experienced with his family, but he has also been intentional in forging relationships with White community members and has established some fruitful relationships. He has listened to people who look different and think differently from him, and he has earned some people's respect and friendship in the process. Granted, this is not something he is required to do, especially if he is being mistreated, but since he is pastoring a church in this community, he has taken it on himself to learn the minds and hearts of those he is proximate with in his community while serving those he can.

Here I should offer a brief caveat. Sometimes situations can be toxic and we need to leave, because a part of antiracist work involves resisting all forms of White supremacy. I decided to leave that predominantly White church where I was on staff because that environment had proven to be very toxic for me and the work that I felt God called me to. I must say this because it's hard to find healing in places of harm, especially if those places are grounded theologically and ideologically in White supremacy. Safe spaces provide an environment where we can heal and work through the injustices we face.

But assuming the steps you take are appropriate, my friend will often tell me, there is power in putting yourself in spaces where you have the opportunity to forge friendships and relationships. This brings us back to the importance of understanding our buried history together. Engaging communities and building strong relationships with others requires a commitment to understanding, and it doesn't happen overnight. Sometimes, our best efforts to be vulnerable and reach out can be met with hidden motives and agendas.

I realize being part of a diverse community, such as I am in today, is not an option for some people. There are often income, social, and relational barriers that make it tough for people to live in a diverse community. Along with this, as much as I'd like to live in a perfect world where there is integration in everything we do, and we all learn to appreciate and value our differences, I realize this is not practical. For example, if you're a White person who lives in an all-White community, you may not have opportunity to meet people from various backgrounds. Likewise, your job, family obligations, and church commitments might make it tougher than you would like to develop strong relationships with people of color, despite having a heart to be proximate in other ways. It's easy for me to call people to action, but I also recognize that not everyone is wired the way I'm wired, and not everyone has had the same opportunities I have.

But here is my challenge: do something.

This might involve a radical step of faith where you say goodbye to some of the comforts you've had in the past and transition into a community that stretches the boundaries of your comfort. Or this journey might start with some small steps such as reading more books by Black authors and other authors of color to decenter ways you have thought in the past before you feel ready to start developing stronger relationships with people of color.

Regardless of where you find yourself today, be intentional in putting good rhythms in place in your life. Change up your pace of life to include people who think, look, and act differently from you.

THE RHYTHM OF JESUS

For Jesus, engaging communities wasn't a one-off event. It was a lifestyle. It was part of his communal nature. I often recall Christ's words in Matthew 25:40: "Whatever you did for one of the least of these brothers and sisters of mine, you did for me." Jesus reminds us that loving people is most important—no matter what social location they emerge from—and that when we focus on loving people, we are bringing glory to God and standing with people in the process.

But for me, the major takeaway from Matthew 25 is the way Jesus commends and speaks to the first group of people who loved others, even when they did not know they were doing so to Christ. Notice Jesus' words when he says in verses 37-39, "Then the righteous will answer him, 'Lord, when did we see you hungry and feed you, or thirsty and give you something to drink? When did we see you a stranger and invite you in, or needing clothes and clothe you? When did we see you sick or in prison and go to visit you?'" In other words, the group of people Jesus is referencing were so committed to loving others and standing with people in suffering that they couldn't even recall when they had loved people in the way Christ described. It was part of who they were. It was a rhythm.

This is how we should live. We should engage the community, and it should be so much of a rhythm of our lives that we aren't even aware we're doing it because it's a normal expression of our love for Christ. This is how we need to think of combating racial injustice in our communities. Our love for God and others should be so strong that we naturally confront injustice whenever we see it and stand for the marginalized even when others are silent.

BRING HEAVEN TO EARTH

Last year I was asked to speak at a conference by the Christian Community Development Association, founded by John Perkins and many others. This conference brings together people from all walks of life who share a desire for social justice.

When I arrived at the conference and looked around at the people from all walks of life—people who were Black, Asian, African, Latinx, Indigenous, White, and so forth—my heart rejoiced. We all came together to worship God and to ask ourselves how we could better show up in the world and represent Christ.

That first night, I sat in one of the main sessions and enjoyed a variety of worship songs that spanned the globe. There were songs in Spanish, Afrikaans, and Indigenous languages. It was as if every person on earth were represented in that auditorium, and I had a small taste of what heaven will one day be like. Even though I didn't recognize or understand all the music, my spirit worshiped God as we celebrated all we had in common. This did something for me.

There was a bookstore at the conference where I and other authors and speakers interacted with attendees. It was great to talk to people from all walks of life. I knew people had different experiences, but it was beautiful to share my experience and hear the stories of others. We found common ground, this drew us closer, and it left me feeling like I was part of a group with different experiences. It was a moment that spoke to me about the type of solidarity we need in our world.

It made me think about what could be. I often think of King's reference to Sunday morning as being the most segregated time of the week as communities of like-minded individuals gather together and worship a God over all nations. It does not have to be this way.

There are some who look at the racial challenges that divide America today and are prone to throw up their hands. The challenges are too great and the price to pay for speaking out too high. But my encouragement to you is to start where you are and to do something. It might be small, but play your role in bringing God's beloved community to earth. Engaging communities can be messy. It's hard work. It doesn't always go as planned. And it takes consistency, sacrifice, and introspection.

ENGAGE LIKE JESUS

Growing up in a Black neighborhood in southwest Atlanta, I was twenty-eight before I really began considering having conversations with the majority White culture. I had attended a Black high school, and all my young adult friends were Black. These experiences shaped my understanding of the world. But my education exposed me to other parts of the world and gave me a fuller understanding of reality. Within a short period of time, I had a brand-new network of friends from all different backgrounds. To be honest, at first this felt very overwhelming.

My first times establishing White friendships and working at a White church were difficult. There was so much I didn't know, and I'll never forget my first experience speaking to an all-White audience. One of my good friends, Jeffrey Roth, asked me to speak at his national youth conference, and as I walked out to the podium to give the first of three messages, I knew things were different.

Instead of the responses I was used to getting in a Black church after a few words, my first words were met with a deafening silence. No one said a word. They just sat and stared. To me, this was strange, but I soon realized it had nothing to do with their form of worship being wrong or mine right. It was just different. And the only way I could better establish friendships was by engaging with these differences and meeting people where they were.

In other words, I had to be more like Jesus. In John 4, Jesus meets a woman from Samaria. There are three reasons this encounter should never have taken place. First, she and Jesus should never have been allowed to cross paths. Jesus was a Jewish man, and Jews hated Samaritans because Samaritans were half-Jewish and half-Gentile, and few Jews passed through Samaria. Second, because of her gender it was considered unlawful for Jesus to engage her in this way. In an era when a woman's testimony would not hold up in court, women were viewed as inferior to men. Jesus embodied what it meant to cross lines and uplift women. The third reason is that she was seen as immoral. The text says she had been married five times and carried a great deal of shame; even her own people despised her. But for Jesus she mattered more than her past and all of the lines that were drawn around this encounter.

Consider their interaction. They are speaking at a well, a common gathering place at the time, the modern equivalent of a coffee shop. Jesus does the unthinkable and asks her for a drink of water. It's unthinkable because he treats her as a person who is worthy of being affirmed. As they speak, the Samaritan woman turns to Jesus and says,

> "You are a Jew and I am a Samaritan woman. How can you ask me for a drink?" (For Jews do not associate with Samaritans.)
>
> Jesus answered her, "If you knew the gift of God and who it is that asks you for a drink, you would have asked him and he would have given you living water."
>
> "Sir," the woman said, "you have nothing to draw with and the well is deep. Where can you get this living water? Are you greater than our father Jacob, who gave us the well and drank from it himself, as did also his sons and his livestock?"
>
> Jesus answered, "Everyone who drinks this water will be thirsty again, but whoever drinks the water I give them will never thirst. Indeed, the water I give them will become in them a spring of water welling up to eternal life." (vv. 9-14)

Notice what happens. Rather than focusing on all they did not have in common, Jesus saw through these differences and looked at the woman for who she was: someone created in the image of God. He didn't allow written history, oral history, or cultural tradition to define their relationship. Instead, he broke through the divide, leaving her to exclaim to onlookers in John 4:29, "Come, see a man who told me everything I ever did."

Almost the totality of Jesus' ministry was spent engaging people of different communities. He modeled what it meant to live in service to others. And he showed us that real engagement equals proximity and service, not distance and apathy. If you are a person of a majority culture, I ask you to pause and think deeply about what has kept you from engaging Black people or people of color in this way. I also ask you to reflect on what lines have been drawn in your mind that cause you to keep away. One of the first steps for us to engage people who are different is to understand there might be barriers that we must cross to stand in solidarity with others to honor God. Jesus honored God in this way with this woman.

APPLICATION

Engaging our communities only happens as we open ourselves up to the challenges those in our communities are facing. It's going back to 1 Corinthians 12:24-26 and caring for others who are made in the image of God. It's recognizing the unique burdens they bear and being willing to help lift the load. More important, it's identifying the barriers and lines that have kept us from engaging people who are different from us.

If you are struggling to engage your whole community, try partnering with others who already are engaged. Don't reinvent the wheel unless you need to. Chances are there are others in your neighborhood who share your passion to engage and are probably already doing the work. What if you joined them? Sat in on a group? Offered your hands in service in a tangible way? As you partner with them, you become stronger, and your vision becomes sustainable.

PRACTICE PROXIMITY

Julia Webb first came to Love Beyond Walls in the latter part of 2016. We were a small organization, and at that point I was still doing much of the behind-the-scenes work to keep us afloat. But as my responsibilities increased, I realized I needed an executive assistant and put out a call on social media. Through a friend of a friend, Julia saw my post and contacted me about the position.

Upon meeting her, I learned a little about her history, upbringing, and social location. She was White and was raised in a White suburban neighborhood that in her words held traditional conservative views about women and BIPOC communities. It was a bubble that felt suffocating. Becoming an executive assistant at Love Beyond Walls would be a big step and different from all she had known and been around for many years of her life, but she was willing to give it a try. Her warm spirit, eagerness, and willingness to step outside her bubble felt like the perfect fit, so I hired her on the spot.

The first few weeks were a bit of an adjustment as she was learning what it was like to be in a space that respected her voice as a woman, and I genuinely wanted to hear what she had to say. Because Julia grew up in a conservative environment, sometimes she felt unqualified for her role as she struggled to connect in a new place with faces and stories she had not been around before. But she was determined to lean in to a new way of showing up in the world and standing with others in solidarity.

I remember mentioning this to one of my long-term staff members, Dexter Culbreath, and we made a collective effort to build her up and call out her strengths. Being from a background where women didn't have much of a voice and were expected to remain home to take care of the family, Julia felt a bit awkward taking on the role of a leader simply because her social location did not afford her many opportunities to be what God designed her to be: a leader. Now, I am in no way saying she wasn't a leader; I'm saying that she had not been given space to be what she already was.

After a few months, I noticed a dramatic change in her. As Julia built community connections, took on new leadership roles, and better understood the world of her new community, she began to identify with people because they were no longer just people, they were friends, and some became family. She saw and interacted with people who were unhoused, people from different walks of life, and folks who were a different skin color from her all-White neighborhood. And rather than allowing her discomfort to push her away, she leaned in and became one of Love Beyond Walls' strongest leaders.

Every day, she made the one-hour commute from her home in the suburbs to our downtown location. Working at a nonprofit organization, she wasn't making a whole lot of money, but she was committed to being proximate. And as she deepened this commitment, Julia's outlook on life shifted. She handled confrontations and learned through interactions with others to confront some of her points of privilege and leveraged her voice to speak up on behalf of those she found new relationships with. She learned the value of affirming all God's children.

Because of her dedication and passion, Julia changed the way her entire family thought about race relationships, poverty, and systemic injustice. Soon after the launch of our Dignity Museum, Julia came to me and said she felt like she was supposed to go back to school and get a degree in mental health counseling. Knowing her as I did, I could tell this was something right in her lane. A few weeks later she transitioned from Love Beyond Walls into her new role as a student. But even after she left, the lessons she learned remained.

I asked Julia to share why proximity was such a powerful concept to her. She responded:

> Proximity has changed everything for me. A person experiencing homelessness or poverty is no longer just a nameless face in a group of nameless faces. They could be Karl or Joe or Rose or Millie or Virgil or Kenny. They were individuals with souls who became dear friends with arms that would give the best hugs and bodies that got cold at night. They became friends I worried about on stormy nights and friends I looked forward to seeing and laughed with and cried with.

Julia's words make me tear up as I read them. They're powerful and they represent how proximity is a two-way street. She reflects further on how proximity was life changing for her as a White woman:

> When I was in my "safe" and homogenized bubble away from the city, I never even had the chance to be in close

proximity with individuals who were different than I was. But putting myself in the position to be close to friends who were facing such overwhelming challenges changed everything. There are some things that cannot be cultivated in a sterile, separate environment. But drawing near to my friends experiencing poverty and homelessness has been a pivotal shift in how I see the world. I recognize that the way I have always known is not the way most other people in the world know. Seeing the world through my friends' eyes changed my fundamental understanding and assumptions about our community, country, and world.

Finally, Julia highlights how being proximate to people changed her:

I am no longer the same. I understand differently. I listen and learn more humbly. I vote differently. I speak differently. I serve differently. I parent differently. And I don't ever want to go back to the "old" me who thought everyone had access to the same things I do. Turns out I was the one living in poverty—poverty of spirit.

Proximity. Changes. Everything.

Not only did Julia offer members of this new community support and encouragement, but through these interactions she also grew as a person, experienced encouragement, and grew in her understanding of her role in advocacy.

PROXIMITY TO PAIN

Julia's life was changed because she made herself proximate to both the best sides of others and their pain. I am not saying that proximity will solve all structural racism, classism, and the myriad ways that White supremacy shows up in the world, but I am saying that full immersion into the lives of people not like us is a huge first step to standing with people in a way that is affirming. We are changed as we learn ways that other people see the world.

This is a point we are prone to forget in an age where any discussion of topics such as critical race theory is often met with fierce opposition, even when those who oppose it don't understand what it is or how it functions. For instance, Black and Brown people who have been unfairly treated by the legal system prompted Black lawyers and scholars to critically examine how race plays a factor in the justice system. However, many White people do not know the background of critical race theory. The NAACP Legal Defense Fund defines it this way:

> Critical Race Theory, or CRT, is an academic and legal framework that denotes that systemic racism is part of American society—from education and housing to employment and healthcare. Critical Race Theory recognizes that racism is more than the result of individual bias and prejudice. It is embedded in laws, policies and institutions that uphold and reproduce racial inequalities. According to CRT, societal issues like Black Americans' higher mortality rate, outsized exposure to police violence, the school-to-prison pipeline, denial of affordable housing, and the rates of the death of Black women in childbirth are not unrelated anomalies.[1]

Proximity matters not only to people but to the history that affects people.

In 2022 the Florida Department of Education shared on its website that they rejected fifty-four mathematics textbooks for its K-12 curriculum because the board felt that it contained CRT material. The sad part is that many of these books were math texts, and math is a subject that is normally not known for containing historic information. However, the Florida Department indicated that the

> Commissioner of Education Richard Corcoran approved Florida's initial adoption list for mathematics instructional materials properly aligned to Florida's Benchmarks for Excellent Student Thinking (B.E.S.T.) Standards. The approved list followed a thorough review of submissions at the Department, which found 41 percent of the submitted textbooks were impermissible with either Florida's new standards or contained prohibited topics—the most in Florida's history. Reasons for rejecting textbooks included references to Critical Race Theory (CRT), inclusions of Common Core, and the unsolicited addition of Social Emotional Learning (SEL) in mathematics. The highest number of books rejected were for grade levels K-5, where an alarming 71 percent were not appropriately aligned with Florida standards or included prohibited topics and unsolicited strategies."[2]

These fifty-four comprised 41 percent of the 132 books submitted. Twenty-eight of these were rejected because they "incorporate prohibited topics or unsolicited strategies, including [critical race theory]."[3]

Some might throw up their hands and say, "What's the big deal? If some states want to ban CRT, why should that matter to us?" But I would point back to James Cone. In *The Cross and the Lynching Tree*, James Cone, a distinguished theologian and scholar, wrote a text to draw a comparative analysis between the suffering Jesus experienced on the cross under Roman rule and the lynching tree that was used by White Southern Americans filled with racial hatred to punish Black people. What is interesting as I read Cone's work is that it unpacked how the cross was used as a symbol of torture, shame, humiliation, violence, and suffering for insurrectionists, rebels, and criminals underneath the Roman Empire; Cone connects that to how Black bodies hung from trees in America in action motivated by the same type of violence and torture that killed an innocent man named Jesus. As he reflects that the cross and the lynching tree are separated by over two thousand years, one is used by the Christian faith in a redemptive way to communicate hope, forgiveness, and salvation; the other—the lynching tree—signified White supremacy and oppression. As Cone recalls in his book,

> Lynching was an extra-legal punishment sanctioned by the community. Many scholars date its origin in Virginia during the Revolutionary War when Charles Lynch or William Lynch (both were called the original "Judge Lynch") . . . punished Tory sympathizers. . . . Lynching as primarily mob violence and torture directed against blacks began to increase after the Civil War and the end of slavery, when the 1867 Congress passed the Reconstruction Act granting black men the franchise and citizenship rights of participation in the affairs of government.[4]

Cone also raises the point that as Jesus' crucifixion was public, so were Black lynchings that drew crowds of White people who brought their families, including children, to see Black people hanged for being Black. These public lynchings became so popular among White families that newspapers even printed ads in the newspapers about when these lynchings would take place. I am an Atlanta native and find it heartbreaking that the *Atlanta Constitution*, as Cone notes, contributed to this. After these public lynchings, White families and individuals would bring their cameras and take pictures of Black bodies hanging from these trees, place them on postcards, and mail them to other family members as keepsakes.[5]

This is part of our shared American history, and when we attempt to bury this ugliness, we fail to understand our current context. We must know our history because it shapes us in many ways. In this specific instance of lynchings, history is a reminder of how many White Americans used the killings of Black bodies to even profit from postcards being sold of this public brutal punishment. This was a part of the history that is not taught and is important for us to recall—when whiteness was treated as superior and blackness was treated as worthless.

Knowing this type of history should serve as a reminder of how far we've come, but also remind us how much work we have to do to create a better pathway forward for those generations coming behind us. Becoming proximate to people is one part, but we should also become proximate to other people's history as the next step to building a heart of solidarity.

When I think of theories like CRT, I do not do so without understanding what prompted a theory like this to be needed. With a little scholarly research, I found out that CRT examines how race and racism can impact people of color in society and the justice system. CRT highlights how people drew a line between the inferiority of Black people and the superiority of White people and how this has been assumed as a part of the social structure in the treatment of Blacks.[6] CRT simply tracks the process of change when Blacks were treated like cattle and seeks to understand what prohibits full equality even to this day.

As a Christian when I see theories like this, I do not run from them; I ask how this could give me a lens to see inequities, injustice, and inequalities differently in our world. Instead of ignoring or attacking theories, believers could be moved like Jesus to see how the gospel might be used to address this type of systemic suffering in our world. If the gospel truly means that all people should be considered worthy and loved by God, how might we be motivated to allow these types of studies to move us to push past racial differences and push us to be proximate with solidarity?

I mention CRT not to push a political agenda but to illustrate the importance of cognitive proximity. This same ban on CRT has been used to ban the teaching of MLK Jr. speeches and letters in certain parts of the country. One of the agendas for framing this field of scholarship as problematic is to distance people from Black history. Being proximate is not just about physical closeness to a person. Real proximity is all-inclusive and includes the desire to understand the full history of people before us, not just those parts we find comfortable. Thus, when political leaders come out in opposition to topics such as CRT, they are calling Americans to distance themselves from their past. They are ignoring the proximity America has had with racial injustice and creating a culture that will only widen the racial divide.

A PROXIMATE THEOLOGY

Jesus' life was marked by proximity. John 1:14 says the Word (Jesus) "became flesh and made his dwelling among us." Choosing not to remain at a distance, Jesus descended into the messiness of humanity and subjected himself to the pains and hardships every human experiences, even to the point of a public death, shame, and suffering for all to witness. Jesus was born into poverty, yet he was still proximate to the poor, women, the disabled, and those considered social outcasts. Jesus' life and ministry personified what it means to live out theology through proximity. His life and witness even baffled people who identified as Jewish.

To Jewish people, the very ones who anticipated a messiah, the manner in which Jesus arrived caught them by surprise. Here was not an instant savior who would deliver them from

Roman oppression, a smooth-talking political figure who would be a friend to the religious elites or some clever military strategist who would rally together a great army. Instead, what they got was a child born into the humblest of situations: a Savior born into poverty in a manger.

We see how God was at work through Jesus in the way that God allowed him to arrive in these humble conditions, with all the inadequacies and vulnerabilities that came with being human in first-century Israel. Yet despite Jesus' humble arrival, he was still an all-knowing, all-powerful, and all-present Savior. And while Jesus was a man without sin, he was also a person who wept when his friend died and sympathized and empathized with those who hurt. Jesus touched lepers who were unclean, ate with sinners, and spoke one-on-one with people like Nicodemus instead of only speaking to people like himself.

The picture of Jesus we see in the four Gospels tells us much about the heart of God. God cared about proximity. Unlike those who believe God set the laws of nature in place and left the universe to operate without his intervention, those who follow Jesus believe in a God who is intimately connected with human affairs. They believe in a God who is proximate to his creation.

In fact, Jesus' entire ministry spanned little more than a twelve-mile radius. While those he commissioned would take the message of the gospel to the ends of the earth, his focus was on a relatively small, globally insignificant, rural area of the world. In many respects, his ministry was the exact opposite of many models we see today that tell Christian leaders to start with the centers of power and allow this influence to trickle down to communities in need. Jesus went to those who had much need, lived among them, sweated with them, conversed with them, and broke bread with them every day.

Even in the last few hours before his death, Jesus was proximate. He had an intimate last supper with his disciples where he warned them of what the next few hours would hold. Then he had an intimate time of prayer in the Garden of Gethsemane with Peter, James, and John. When Judas, his betrayer, came, he greeted him with a kiss. And when Simon Peter took out his sword and slashed off the ear of the high priest's servant, Malchus, Jesus picked up the ear and healed the very man who was sent to arrest him.

Jesus was proximate, and he was present from birth till death.

PROXIMITY DEFINED

Back in 2011, my friend Bob Lupton wrote *Toxic Charity*, in which he explored ways churches can hurt the people they want to help. I had a chance to interview him for a documentary our organization produced at Love Beyond Walls called *Voiceless*. It's a film that shares the stories of those who are impoverished to get a better understanding about what is happening across the country, and he shared a story of becoming familiar with the term *gentrification*.

Bob is an older White gentleman, a psychologist, and he would consider himself a person of privilege. Before moving to Atlanta, Bob had never heard the term *gentrification*. Bob and his wife bought a piece of land in a more rundown area where there had not been new construction for around sixty years. Most of the homes surrounding them were old and worn. Many times, they were rented out to lower-income families. But after building his home, Bob noticed a trend emerging. Home after home around them underwent renovation. Sometimes this involved tearing the entire house down and starting from scratch. Initially Bob was grateful because he knew the property value of his home would rise.

But his joy was short lived. At his neighborhood church, Bob started to overhear others in the community make statements like, "Please pray for me. They've just doubled my rent," or, "Please pray for me. They're putting the house I rent on the market to sell." Through these conversations and living in proximity to his neighbors, Bob realized that what was benefiting him was not beneficial to many of his neighbors. He says, "I was getting richer, while my neighbors were getting poorer."[7]

Bob had no clue how the poor were hurt by gentrification until he worshiped with people who were praying about their rent in that neighborhood. As I said in my book *When We Stand*, "Embracing proximity is not only the means by which we get closer to real-life issues but also how we enter into and develop deep relationships that could be beneficial to our own lives as we seek to achieve justice in the world."[8] And today, those words ring truer than ever in my ears: "Accepting the need to live in proximity to others is how you become seen as an individual—as well as being, in turn, the way in which you have a chance to see and affirm the dignity of others. Being in proximity to people is how we connect with others to seek justice and change the world. Jesus connected with people to whom he was proximate, so why would it be any different for us?"[9]

PROXIMITY THAT ACKNOWLEDGES THE REAL ISSUES

One of the reasons we don't live in proximity with others is a failure to acknowledge the issues that drive us apart. As the Reverend William Barber notes, "One of the problems with the way we do American analysis is we act as though there is not a past to connect it to the present."[10] Instead, we bury aspects of our shameful history that include Reconstruction, the Southern Strategy, and redlining and act as though these did not create a structure that makes it more difficult for Black Americans to thrive.

In *Four Hundred Souls*, Barber writes, "Though slavery officially ended after the Civil War, the Christianity that blessed White supremacy did not go away. It doubled down on the Lost Cause, endorsed racial terrorism during the Redemption era, blessed the leaders of Jim Crow, and continues to endorse racist policies as traditional values under the guise of a 'religious right.'"[11] Many White political leaders—many professing to be Christian—have grown adept at using language that disguises their racism. Instead of using the N-word, they use code words such as "entitlements" and "tax reform."

This needs to change. According to Barber, "We need a Moral Movement across the nation. An indigenously homegrown, state-based, state government-focused, deeply moral, deeply constitutional, anti-racist, anti-poverty, pro-justice, pro-labor, transformative, Fusion Movement. A Movement that is about the moral fabric of our society guided by a deeply moral and constitutional vision of what is possible."[12]

From Barber's perspective, these movements do not begin with any political party. Rather, movements can motivate Black, Brown, Indigenous, old, young, housed, unhoused, White, and others to unite to spur political leaders and parties into positive action. He calls it a fusion of people standing with one another. This is what I call solidarity work and the power of affirming all God's children. Put another way, the solution to dealing with many of the macro racial problems in America starts at a micro level as we live in close proximity to others. What we need instead is an attitude of proximity and to cultivate what Felicia Song calls faithful presence. She writes:

> Faithful presence, therefore, looks little like a mild-mannered desire to avoid going against the grain in order to retain some semblance of middle-class decency. Rather, faithful presence is made of steely commitment and

sacrificial love that often bucks the social norm. Faithful presence might look like staying put when everyone in their right mind is packing up to leave. Faithful presence might look like coming together to tend to one's neighbors, even at the risk of one's own security.[13]

Presence is about deep connection and relationships. It's more about being than it is doing.[14]

WHY WE STRUGGLE TO SEE THOSE AROUND US

Back when I was ten, my grandmother Jessica Lester noticed me squint my eyes several times one evening and suggested my mom take me to the eye doctor. After a series of tests, I found out I was nearsighted. I could see things within ten feet of my nose, but anything beyond that started to get blurry. Before this test, I had just assumed the way I saw the world paralleled everyone else's viewing experience. Little did I know.

When I think of the church and the topic of race, I think one of our major challenges has been our historical nearsightedness. We notice people right before our eyes, but we either fail to place ourselves in geographical proximity to those who are different, or fail to see the big picture of their lives and how they connect to human history. Either way, the result is that we miss what's really going on.

But living a genuine life of racial proximity means we take note of the macro and micro challenges of those with ethnic backgrounds different from ours. We take a farsighted approach and notice those who look different from us, then we position ourselves in proximity to them and look at their daily joys and the challenges they experience. In doing so, we allow our in-person interactions to shape our big picture understanding of groups and communities we previously misunderstood. Doing so requires us to act like my friend Julia, stepping out of our comfort zones, seeing with open eyes, and living alongside those who have had different life experiences.

Historically, the church in America has been quite near-sighted when it comes to matters of racial injustice. It's easy for a White church member in nice suburban communities to watch right-leaning media and gain a blurry picture of the real struggles Black people face. As a result, they become near-sighted and import their experience of Black culture as the entire experience of a group of people they do not understand. Nearsighted thinkers don't want their views to be challenged. They are content with their picture being blurry from a distance. When this happens, Professor Travis Dixon notes, "this leaves people with the opinion that Black people are plagued with self-imposed dysfunction that creates family instability and therefore, all their problems."[15] In a study Dixon conducted of those who watched the news, he found that "news and opinion media overrepresent poor families as being Black and underrepresent poor families as being White."[16]

But real understanding requires a change in vision, and that can happen with proximity, which then lays the foundation of standing in solidarity with other people.

Not long ago, my eleven-year-old son received his first pair of glasses. Like his dad, he is nearsighted and needs something to help him to see objects far away. And after trying them on for the first time, he had this awkward mix of embarrassment and excitement. While he liked the look and feel of wearing glasses, he was a little worried at what others would think.

This is one of the biggest challenges we face with race in our country. Most people say they want to see clearly and get to a place where racial division is not an issue. But the lack of confronting history keeps White people blind and unable to stand in solidarity with BIPOC people. The only way we get there is by going through the nervous, uncomfortable phase of putting on the glasses, understanding our history, and taking both a broad and a narrow look at our buried history.

APPLICATION

Proximity is powerful and can happen in many different forms, but while some might argue that they do not need to be proximate to people who may emerge from a different social location, geographical proximity can be life changing, as we see displayed in the life of Jesus. Being proximate to actual people can help you see the pain in someone's eyes, notice how others might respond to a policy problem differently, and give you an understanding of how the person before you is a real person. All of these can cause you to change and learn how the world might be seen by someone different from you and move you to stand with that person against any injustice that might be threatening their life. Reverend Barber calls this a "fusion."

William Barber talks about the five key interlocked areas of systematic racism, poverty, ecological devastation, the war economy, and the false narrative of Christian nationalism and White evangelicalism.[17] Tackling any one of these issues requires us to look at all five. This tells us that proximity isn't just about doing lip service or standing in close physical distance to others but rolling up our sleeves and tackling the real issues that break us apart and oppress others.

How are you placing yourself in proximity to others? How are you standing with them in solidarity? Is it with the desire to build meaningful relationships?

SIT AT ANOTHER'S TABLE

Have you ever sat at a table and felt like you did not belong? Maybe you were invited to a coworker's birthday party, only to arrive and realize everyone else knew each other except you. Everyone was swapping stories about blasts from the past while you sat there in silence, trying to add your two cents every few minutes, knowing your life experiences do not parallel those of everyone else in the room. It's an exhausting experience, especially if you're an introvert like me. By the end of the evening you're ready to escape to the comfort of familiar surroundings.

In 2015, I had an encounter like this. It was a warm, sunny afternoon as I walked into a Panera Bread in the suburbs of Atlanta for my first meeting as part of the staff at a White church. I was new to the church staff, and I was the only Black person at the table. In fact, I was the only person of color in the entire restaurant, and as I sat down and spoke with fellow staff members, I could sense the eyeballs staring in my direction.

The unspoken message was clear: *What is this Black guy doing at an all-White table?*

Prior to this meeting, I had had several conversations with the leadership of the church and was excited about their verbal commitment to diversity and inclusion. And as I walked in and sat down, these same individuals greeted me with smiles and kind words. But as the meeting started, my excitement began to subside, and I realized the real reason I was there. I was seated at this table to check the diversity box on the church staff and to offer suggestions about situations or programs that might offend people of color. That was it.

My suspicions were confirmed only a few minutes into the meeting when I suggested we diversify our music style to include Black gospel music. This initial idea was quickly dismissed, but I tried again a few minutes later, speaking about the importance of not just having a "White Jesus" on the Power-Point slides at church and diversifying our imagery so people of all skin colors felt affirmed. As before, the leaders were polite but were also quick to dismiss my opinions with little more than a passing comment about why this would never work in their context. This happened over and over and over. Before long, I just sat in silence. I was invited to sit at the table, but only as an empty shell.

The whole situation felt like a bait and switch. I was invited to be on the team, but only as the water boy. I could speak up when asked and assist those who were actually doing the ministry, but I could not take a real position. It's one thing to invite others to sit at your table. But it's a whole different matter to lay aside your privilege and power and fully share space at the table, especially with Black people and people of color. Doing so requires humility and the willingness to learn from others who might hold opinions different from yours.

The problem I faced that warm afternoon is similar to the challenge so many Black people face today when they are invited to sit at the tables, only to be there as decoration. We are invited to participate in the conversation, but we aren't given the opportunity to share our full expression. We are asked to speak, but we do so with muzzles over our mouths.

Having the opportunity to speak at a table but not being permitted to use your full voice is a degrading experience. You feel unheard and unseen. And as MLK Jr. famously stated, "A riot is the language of the unheard."[1] When enough people feel their voices do not matter, they eventually stand up and say, "Enough is enough."

I believe the intentions were good when I was first offered a seat at the table of a White congregation. The lead pastor wanted to shift his focus and wanted me to handle a number of outreach initiatives and reach folks in impoverished communities. But gradually my seat at the table was diminished. I wasn't included in the same conversations I had been privy to in the past, and my voice was silenced when it came to speaking up about bothersome things that could be racially offensive. I recognized just how harmful a seat at the table could become when racial issues are not addressed.

When I first started going to staff meetings, I would sit at this long conference table with each of the other members of our team. Many days, it didn't feel like I had much of a voice in this conversation. I was asked to speak up if the topic revolved around race relations, but I felt most of my other opinions were easily dismissed. I was asked to say something if I heard anything that sounded offensive to people of color. This struck me as odd because I didn't sign up to be a pastor at a church to police harmful phrases or anything that came across as offensive. I signed up to be part of the family of God.

There were microaggressions every day. The lyrics of Black musicians were referenced in staff meetings in a derogatory fashion, as though Black music was inferior to White music. They were keen to tip a hat to Black culture without giving it the respect it deserved. There was a White woman who often touched my hair in staff meetings and would make statements like, "Your hair is so well kept!" Others said I was very articulate for a person of color. Looking back, I don't know why I allowed myself to be mistreated in a way God would never want me to endure because I, too, am a part of God's family.

I remember walking into a staff meeting and the White worship leader saying, "What up, dog?" It was as if he wanted to engage my Black culture, but the only way he knew how was through using street slang. To me, it was his way of engaging as best he understood with Black culture and reducing me to what he thought I would relate to. He wouldn't have thought of addressing notable Black figures such as Oprah Winfrey or Barack Obama with that type of lingo, but he felt it was suitable for me.

Understand that it wasn't the words that stung the most. For example, when someone walked up to me and said, "What up, Big T?" I wasn't offended by this term. Rather, it was the way it was used and the unspoken meaning behind it. I am not sure he knew how offensive this was, but to the Black person it can feel as though we are being viewed as less in the mind of someone White.

It didn't matter that my two master's degrees meant I had more education than anyone else on staff. It didn't matter that I have a huge library, that I'm a voracious reader, and that Black hip-hop music was just one small part of my life's mosaic. It didn't matter that I was a gifted communicator. The microaggressions continued.

There are three forms of microaggression: microassaults, microinvalidation, and microinsults. Derald Sue and colleagues write:

> Racial microaggressions are brief and commonplace daily verbal, behavioral, and environmental indignities, whether intentional or unintentional, that communicate hostile, derogatory, or negative racial slights and insults to the target person or group. They are not limited to human encounters alone but may also be environmental in nature, as when a person of color is exposed to an office setting that unintentionally assails his or her racial heritage or identity. . . . Microinsults represent subtle snubs, frequently unknown to the perpetrator, but clearly convey a hidden insulting message to the recipient of color. . . . Microinsults can also occur nonverbally, as when a White teacher fails to acknowledge students of color in the classroom or when a White supervisor seems distracted during a conversation with a Black employee by avoiding eye contact or turning away (Hinton, 2004). In this case, the message conveyed to persons of color is that their contributions are unimportant.[2]

There were many times when I would speak up about themes I thought we needed to cover in upcoming services or ways we needed to engage our communities. But each time, my ideas were shot down or casually dismissed. Oddly, there were many times another White member of our team would make the exact point I had just made, and their idea would be accepted.

The leaders of this church had little interest in empowering Black people; they wanted instead to have a false representation of multiculturalism and diversity.

MORE THAN DIVERSITY

After these meetings, I would sit in my car and ask myself, *What is going on? Why am I allowing myself to go through this?* I felt alone because other people on staff couldn't relate to me. I felt uncomfortable speaking up because I wasn't one of the primary leaders. I felt alone and as though I was only on the staff for appearances.

Supposedly just by having me there increased diversity. It was me being given the "privilege" of sitting at an all-White table. Many White people talk of inviting people of color to the table, but the idea is still that they own the table. As Bernice King tweeted, "Even the statement, 'Let's invite more Black people to the table,' implies ownership of the table and control of who is invited. Racism is about power."[3] Rev. Gricel Medina, a Latina pastor, responded to King's tweet with these words, "This is a very painful reality for brown and black leaders. If the table is owned by white and the authority voices are white, then we are nothing more than tokens. If our voices are only present to empower them . . . No thank you!"[4]

Inclusion involves making a full contribution. Inclusion opens the door for expression. Inclusion is a pathway to belonging. It's inviting Black people to sit at the table *and* allowing them to express the totality of who they are—that is true belonging. It is not limiting their ability to be their full selves.

Take the recent discrimination lawsuit by former Miami Dolphins head coach Brian Flores against the NFL, alleging racial bias in the way head coaches are interviewed and given opportunity. The lawsuit states, "This class-action lawsuit was and remains long overdue. The NFL—left to its own devices to police itself—has continually failed to address the massive imbalance and underrepresentation of Black coaches and executives."[5]

Of the thirty-two NFL teams, only two have Black head coaches, and there has never been a Black primary owner.[6] Contrast this with the fact that roughly 70 percent of players in the league are Black. Black players are invited to "sit at the table" and show off their skills on Sunday, but they are often inhibited from having a meaningful voice that sets the tone of the organization and league.

William Rhoden notes in *Forty Million Dollar Slaves: The Rise, Fall, and Redemption of the Black Athlete* that Blacks in America have changed from working at literal plantations to today's figurative ones. He points out how sports function as entertainment to appease White audiences, paralleling a time when Black people were enslaved and their bodies used for the same thing—entertainment. As much as we might like to think things have changed, some of these same discriminatory systems remain today.

Diversity is not enough. Saying "Everyone is welcome" is drastically different from "We built this with you in mind." People don't want to go where they are merely tolerated; they want to go where they are included, because the ultimate goal is to create spaces that center belonging. Building something with others in mind takes intention. Whether you're building a community to include Latinx people, Asian Americans, Indigenous, or African American people, or any people group of color you need to start with the experience of those you plan to center. Remember, people don't want to go where they are merely tolerated; they want to go where they are included.

SITTING AT ANOTHER TABLE

In today's American culture where diversity is celebrated, people are eager to extend a seat at their table. But this invitation often comes with a catch. It allows the inviter to maintain a position of power and to frame the narrative as they choose. This plays out in countless ways. A common example is a Black speaker being invited to join a panel discussion on race at a mostly White congregation. The Black speaker is invited to share their perspective but only on certain questions the interviewer deems important.

While inviting someone to sit at your table can be good, I suggest taking this a step further and sitting at the table of another. If you are a White person, this means placing yourself in contexts where you submit to the leadership of people of color and adopt the posture of a learner. Doing so requires humility, and humility involves teachability. It's assuming the posture of a student by acknowledging that others, regardless of their position in culture, can be our teachers.

This is something I do my best to practice. If I'm walking about and I come across someone who is obviously struggling, I do not position myself as their superior. I check my tone and mannerisms. In part, one of the reasons this comes easier for me than for some is because I remember some of the lowest periods of my life. I remember what it was like when I experienced homelessness as a teenager. I recall the shame I felt and that feeling of never measuring up. And most important, I remember what I was like before I met Jesus. I resonate with the words of Isaiah 64:6 that my "righteous acts are like filthy rags." I was nothing before I met Christ, and I am only something today because I know him. Because this is my story, there is no room to be puffed up and view myself as superior to others.

I think often of these words concerning Jesus in Philippians 2:5-8:

In your relationships with one another, have the same mindset as Christ Jesus:

Who, being in very nature God
  did not consider equality with God something to
    be used to his own advantage;
rather, he made himself nothing
  by taking the very nature of a servant,
  being made in human likeness.
And being found in appearance as a man,
  he humbled himself
  by becoming obedient to death—even death on
    a cross!

Jesus certainly did not need to subject himself to the slings and arrows of a depraved human world. Yet, out of obedience to his Father and his love for the world, he chose the path of greatest humility and highest redemption. He lowered himself so he could raise to life anyone who confessed their sins and placed their hope in him. In the words of psychologist and Christian counselor Diane Langberg:

Because Jesus never wavered from choosing love and obedience to the Father as the driving force in His life, He was a threat to both individuals and systems of His day, a holy dissident with a disruptive presence and disruptive words. His character threatened Rome's powerful ways— warfare, conquering, bloodshed, and oppression. It also threatened the religious system, which exercised power & fostered rigidity, empty ritual, exclusion, & judgment. He who was the foundation of that system looked nothing like it. He opposed all that was contrary to the purposes and character of the Father in individual, social, national, ethnic, and religious life. He sat apart from those who stood together, and in doing so, His faithfulness to the Father led to His extermination . . . or so they thought.[7]

Jesus was born into the poorest conditions. He had no position of power, and the man who did (Herod) was corrupt and a murderer. Jesus' family was displaced at an early age, and he was forced to flee into Egypt with the few possessions he had. As he grew, he suffered public ridicule and was mocked for the community from which he had come. "Can anything good come out of Nazareth?" people wondered. He knew what it meant to experience a lack of belonging.

Even with his astonishing ability to articulate the Hebrew Scriptures and share the truths of God's Word he was constantly challenged, undercut, and viewed with suspicion by the religious leaders of his day. Still, he gave his life for the very people who did not want him to belong. As Howard Thurman noted, "Jesus rejected hatred. It was not because he lacked the vitality or the strength. It was not because he lacked the incentive. Jesus rejected hatred because he saw that hatred meant death to the mind, death to the spirit, death to communion with his Father. He affirmed life; and hatred was the great denial."[8]

Jesus stood for the disadvantaged and sat at the table of others.

HOW DO I SIT WHEN I DON'T UNDERSTAND?

When I raised the idea to the all-White staff of singing more Black gospel songs in church, I did so because I felt that incorporating some of these songs would make Black people feel more at home. Contemporary Christian worship music was fine, but it didn't exactly fit my background, or the background of virtually every Black person in attendance. But once again this idea was shut down. The White worship leader responded, saying, "I can't sing those types of songs." He felt inadequate and unable to relate to a culture and musical genre that was unfamiliar. But what he didn't understand was that it wasn't about him hitting all the notes precisely on point. It was about an opportunity to represent a population that felt unseen and to make it easier for them to worship their risen Savior.

Unfortunately, as Austin Channing Brown remarks, "a great many people believe that reconciliation boils down to dialogue: a conference on race, a lecture, a moving sermon about the diversity we'll see in heaven. But dialogue is productive toward reconciliation only when it leads to action—when it inverts power and pursues justice for those who are most marginalized."[9] As followers of Christ, we should move beyond dialogue and learn what it means to stand in solidarity with others.

This conversation points us back to the importance of understanding. It is critical we understand people's stories about where they have come from and where they are going. This helps us create a culture of solidarity.

Recently, one of my Atlanta friends was at a hotel in Florida. During his time there, he and a few African American bishop colleagues were enjoying lunch. A few minutes after they sat down, a middle-aged White man dressed in shorts and a T-shirt came over and asked why they were there in business casual clothes. When my friend explained the reason for their stay, the White man asked if they had ever voted Republican, offered some lines White evangelicals often say about social justice, and launched into an abortion argument, assuming he knew where my friends stood on the issue.

As my friend shared, this man didn't know his credentials, history, service, pastorate, family, or his love for people. "He was simply looking for an angle to become instructive and paternal as he stood over us."[10] When I read his post, it brought back all these feelings of not being seen and being a demographic grabber for a White church congregation. I remembered what it felt like to sit at the table but not be offered a real voice.

THE FUNNEL OF ACCEPTANCE

Most of the time when people talk about diversity, equity, and inclusion they don't talk about belonging and access. This is because they don't see the problem for what it is. In speaking about some of the horrific racial injustices in American history, Mary-Francis Winters writes, "The truth is that White people are not required to know. As the dominant group, they can go through life with the privilege of never thinking about their race. Many White people still claim not to 'see' race. If you do not see it, there is no reason to address it. You can be sublimely ignorant."[11]

If you look at the path to solidarity like a funnel, diversity is at the top. Everyone wants to be more diverse. Next is equity, which involves being fair and impartial, leveling the playing field to ensure everyone gets equal resources. Lamar Hardwick writes, "Equality is necessary for the gospel to be taken seriously. We cannot seek diversity without unity, and we cannot seek unity without equality."[12] Inclusion takes us further down this funnel, but it still has its limitations.

Belonging is where everything starts to change. Creating belonging is the work of solidarity. Belonging communicates you belong here and I am going to stand with you. It's having your identity affirmed with the understanding that the larger community is blessed to have you as a part. They recognize they are a better place for having someone who is different on board. When you belong, you don't have to always question your status and position in the community. You don't have to worry about saying the wrong thing and being instantly excommunicated.

When you belong, you feel safe and at home. You are for the community, and the community is for you. Belonging suggests that our story belongs in this community, and what shapes us belongs here.

The final position on the funnel is access. This is when we know belonging has taken hold. Access is more than having resources available to all groups. Access incorporates the preferences of others. It's playing music that represents each culture.

WE STAND TODAY BECAUSE OTHERS HAVE SAT

Numerous decent White people have embodied sacrifice and leveraged their position of privilege and power to sit at someone else's table, hear their story, and motivate others to become antiracists:

- Anne McCarty Braden, who was a civil rights activist, journalist, and educator and believed in racial equality and stood against racism, helped a Black couple buy a house in an all-White area of Louisville, Kentucky, in 1954 during Jim Crow and a time when families could have been severely harmed.
- Edgar Chandler was a congregational minister and active leader in the civil rights movement alongside Dr. Martin Luther King Jr.[13] He also helped bring Jesse Jackson into the civil rights movement as stated by Jackson himself.
- Prudence Crandall, who defied racial discrimination and helped run the first known African American school for girls in 1833.
- Jane Elliot, who is an advocate for antiracism and the fair treatment of Black people through her Blue eyes/Brown eyes exercise and public lectures and trainings.
- Eric Kulberg, the photographer responsible for capturing some of the most iconic images from the March on

Washington in 1963. In fact, Kulberg was eighteen years of age when he snapped those photos. The *Washington Post* reported, "Eric Kulberg was an 18-year-old intern in the summer of 1963 when he asked his boss for the day off so he could attend the March on Washington. 'What are you, a n----- lover or something?' Kulberg's superior at the Department of the Interior asked. 'Uh-huh. I guess so,' Kulberg blurted out."[14]

- Mary White Ovington, who was a pioneer of civil rights after hearing Frederick Douglass speak and was one of many cofounders for the NAACP alongside Ida B. Wells, W. E. B. Du Bois, and Moorfield Storey.[15]
- Mr. Fred Rogers, who sought to create a kids' program for people of all backgrounds.[16] According to the *Today Show*, "In a 1993 episode of 'Mister Rogers' Neighborhood,' Rogers invited Officer Clemmons to soak his feet in a wading pool, a reference to a 1969 episode with a similar scene, which aired amid civil unrest over racially segregated pools."[17] This scene was a solidarity stand with a Black man against racial injustice on national television.

And although this is a very short list, there are many more today standing in solidarity with their BIPOC brothers and sisters. As Elizabeth Denevi and Lori Cohen write, "Antiracism for White people is a process of recognizing the impact of race as a system of oppression and engaging in practices, behaviors, and ways of being that disrupt racial discrimination."[18]

The late Rabbi Abraham Joshua Heschel in a classic speech on religion and race offered this profound call to action: "Let there be a grain of prophet in every man! Our concern must be expressed not symbolically, but literally; not only publicly, but also privately; not only occasionally, but regularly. What we need is the involvement of every one of us as individuals. What we need is *restlessness*, a constant awareness of the monstrosity of injustice."[19]

We need men and women who live with a holy sense of discontent, people who are willing to speak up about injustice, invite others to sit at their table, and humble themselves to sit at the feet of another. Sitting at the table of others is important and what solidarity is all about. It's one thing to invite others to sit at your table. But it's a whole different matter to lay aside your privilege and sit at the table of another. Doing so requires humility and the willingness to learn from others who might hold opinions different from yours.

APPLICATION

Fortunately, I've had numerous leaders in my life who have been a positive voice of encouragement and hope. I think of my friend Jerome Lubbe. Jerome had his first debilitating migraine when he was seventeen, and since then he has averaged around a hundred migraines a year. You read that right: one hundred. Many of his days are spent in severe pain where he finds it difficult to function. As a complex neurological patient, Jerome lives in what he describes as "medical purgatory."[20] And it was Jerome's journey of pain that led him to become a functional neurologist and lend his services to others.

On May 14, 2022, my wife and I were involved in a serious car accident. I had multiple bone fractures in my hip and lost the ability to feel my legs. I was scared, and as I lay in the hospital bed with 24/7 medical care, I wondered if I would ever be able to walk again.

This is when Jerome stepped into my life. Jerome is a White South African and understands the complexities of racial tensions in the United States and the access and privilege available in White society. This has only increased his level of empathy and care for others, and when Jerome found out I would need to relearn to walk, he donated his time outside of practice hours to come over to my house every Sunday and work with me to strengthen movement in my legs. He showed up every weekend for months, and my mobility dramatically improved. Because of his efforts, doctors shared that my recovery time was a year ahead of schedule. Jerome literally came to my table and saw me.

Every day, you have the opportunity to be like Jerome or to be someone who uses people of color as tokens to check a diversity box. You can love people for who they are, or you can be patronizing and condescending. The choice is up to you. My suggestion? Choose to be like Jesus, but live to show up practically like Jerome.

CHAPTER TEN

BREAK
THE SILENCE

On March 29, 2022, President Joe Biden signed into law the Emmett Till Anti-lynching Act, which makes lynching a federal hate crime. As Tajma Hall notes, "Since 1900, there have been more than 200 failed attempts to pass anti-lynching laws."[1] But thanks to people like Bryan Stevenson, founder and executive director of the Equal Justice Initiative in Montgomery, Alabama, the reminder of American's dark past was never forgotten. On April 26, 2018, Stevenson helped launch the National Memorial for Peace and Justice, "the nation's first memorial dedicated to the legacy of enslaved Black people, people terrorized by lynching, African Americans humiliated by racial segregation and Jim Crow, and people of color burdened with contemporary presumptions of guilt and police violence."[2]

The story of Emmett Till is gut-wrenching. Born in Chicago, Illinois, fourteen-year-old Emmett was on vacation near Money, Mississippi, on August 24, 1955, when he entered a convenience store and had an encounter with

twenty-one-year-old Carolyn Bryant, the daughter of a plan-
tation manager. After Emmett purchased two cents of gum, the
details of what happened next are unclear. Bryant alleged that
Emmett flirted with her. This enraged Bryant, and she rushed
out of the store. The kids outside said she was going to get
a pistol.

Although he was out of town at the time of the incident,
Bryant's husband returned and learned from one of the kids
about what had happened. As someone who prided himself on
dealing with Blacks, Roy Bryant took matters into his own
hands. At around 2:30 a.m. on August 28, Roy and his half
brother, J. W. Milam, showed up at the home of Moses Wright,
where Emmett was staying. "His assailants—the White
woman's husband and his brother—made Emmett carry a 75-
pound cotton gin fan to the bank of the Tallahatchie River and
ordered him to take off his clothes. The two men then beat him
nearly to death, gouged out his eye, shot him in the head, and
then threw his body, tied to the cotton gin fan with barbed
wire, into the river."[3]

Both Bryant and Milam would go on to be acquitted by an
all-White jury, drawing sympathy and even being portrayed as
mini-celebrities among some in the media. They would eventually confess to their deeds in an interview published in *Look*
magazine in January 1956. On the surface, every appearance
indicated that evil had won.

But this is where one voice would speak up and forever
change the course of history. Mamie Bradley, Emmett's mother,
took one look at the mutilated body she could not even recognize as her son and made a bold decision. Rather than doing
the "respectable" thing, she demanded an open casket viewing
of her boy so that all could see what had been done. More than
five thousand people attended, and his murder became one of
the key points of the civil rights movement.

Mamie Bradley's actions sparked the Montgomery bus boycott, "a civil rights protest during which African Americans refused to ride city buses in Montgomery, Alabama, to protest segregated seating," from December 5, 1955, until December 20, 1956.[4] This protest eventually resulted in the Supreme Court's ruling that segregated seating on buses was unconstitutional.

It's been said that the reason God gives us influence is so that we can speak up for those who have none. Evil can only be disarmed when we are brave enough to step forward and take a risk for the sake of our brothers and sisters. When racial tension occurs, we are presented with a golden opportunity to dismantle the perpetuation of hate and judgment or to further it.

Breaking the silence can be scary and uncomfortable, but it is the way of Jesus.

A JESUS WHO SPEAKS

One of my favorite passages of Scripture is John 12:24. Jesus is speaking of his coming death and makes this profound statement: "Unless a kernel of wheat falls to the ground and dies, it remains only a single seed. But if it dies, it produces many seeds."

The significance of this passage cannot be overstated. It reveals that God can take even the deepest pain, the horror of a barbaric death, and turn it into a movement that brings deliverance for his people. In the hours leading up to his crucifixion, Jesus endured beatings, disfigurement, verbal abuse, and the betrayal of some of his closest friends. Still, the suffering he experienced was worth it for the joy that was set before him (Hebrews 12:2): the joy of heaven, the joy of doing the will of his Father, and the joy of seeing generations enter into relationship with him.

And as much as I like John 12:24, I equally love the verse that follows when Jesus states, "Anyone who loves their life will lose it, while anyone who hates their life in this world will keep it for eternal life." This verse puts the reality of Jesus' death and suffering into perspective for those who want to follow him. It's not enough to say, "I want to be like Christ." Instead, each of us must be willing to take up our cross, deny ourselves, and follow him, even if this may lead us to the point of death.

This reality flies in the face of our Western desire for comfort and safety. It confronts those who remain silent while injustice rages. And it calls to action those who have sat on the sidelines and not engaged. If we want to follow in the footsteps of Jesus, we must be willing to break the silence wherever we go. Consider this passage in John 8:

> The teachers of the law and the Pharisees brought in a woman caught in adultery. They made her stand before the group and said to Jesus, "Teacher, this woman was caught in the act of adultery. In the Law Moses commanded us to stone such women. Now what do you say?" They were using this question as a trap, in order to have a basis for accusing him.
>
> But Jesus bent down and started to write on the ground with his finger. When they kept on questioning him, he straightened up and said to them, "Let any one of you who is without sin be the first to throw a stone at her." Again he stooped down and wrote on the ground.
>
> At this, those who heard began to go away one at a time, the older ones first, until only Jesus was left, with the woman still standing there. Jesus straightened up and asked her, "Woman, where are they? Has no one condemned you?"

"No one, sir," she said.

"Then neither do I condemn you," Jesus declared. "Go now and leave your life of sin."

Jesus faces a seemingly impossible decision. As much as he might sympathize with the woman caught in adultery, the reality is she does stand guilty of violating the law. In that period of history, adultery was no joking matter and was punishable by death. Any self-serving politician in Jesus' shoes would have sat this discussion out. They might have thought to themselves, *Sure, I feel bad for this lady, and it's obvious these religious leaders have an agenda. But there is nothing I can do that's not going to make me look bad and, worse yet, place me in the position of sympathizing with her.* But not Jesus. Instead, he spoke up with words that penetrated the hearts of this woman's condemners. With a simple statement Jesus dispersed the mob, and because he was willing to speak up, a woman's life was spared.

True to his mission, Jesus' actions lived up to the prophet Isaiah's words, quoted in Luke 4:18-19: "The Spirit of the Lord is on me, because he has anointed me to proclaim good news to the poor. He has sent me to proclaim freedom for the prisoners and recovery of sight for the blind, to set the oppressed free, to proclaim the year of the Lord's favor."

Just as Jesus came to proclaim the good news to the poor, oppressed, and disadvantaged, and just as he stepped in to prevent a woman from being stoned, so we should use our voices and our strength to come to the aid of others.

A VOCAL BLACK CHURCH

In 2021, PBS released a four-hour documentary with Henry Louis Gates Jr. on the Black church. This series takes viewers from the transatlantic slave trade through Emancipation, Jim

Crow, the civil rights era, and up to 2021. It demonstrates how the Black church was foundational for holding African Americans together during times of great hardship.

One figure they highlight is James Cone, who said, "God's story is the Black story, and the Black story is God's story. And that is the Christian story."[5] This statement deeply impacted individuals such as Rev. Kelly Brown Douglas of Union Theological Seminary. Hearing this at a point when she felt the need to choose between being Black and being Christian, Cone's statement helped her to understand that Christ stood with those who were oppressed and that the church was for her.

According to Cone, "Black faith emerged out of Black people's wrestling with suffering, the struggle to make sense out of their senseless situation, as they related their own predicament to similar stories in the Bible."[6] This is a faith that was tried, tested, and refined in the fires of adversity. The church became a place where Black folks rose to leadership, and it provided a sense of dignity and worth to Black men and women. In the church, a young Black man who was called a boy outside the four walls of the building was known as a leader within those very walls. And during the '60s, the church became a sacred space and a cornerstone of the civil rights movement. It was the eschatological hope for those who were discouraged. And it urged them to look to a God who would make all things new and right every injustice.

Like Cone, the history of the Black American church is filled with individuals who have spoken up at precisely the right moments, including people like Richard Allen, founder of the African Methodist Episcopal Church, which was the first Black denomination in the United States. Prior to Allen, Black people mostly worshiped in White churches and were thus treated as second-class citizens even in the house of God, at times even being pushed out of the church as they knelt in prayer at the altar. Allen created a church culture where Black people could worship freely. Other examples include Absalom Jones, who cofounded the Free African Society with Richard Allen in 1787, and Jarena Lee, who was the first African American to proclaim the gospel publicly to racially mixed audiences that crossed denominational lines.

The list is almost endless, and illustrates how, instead of declining during seasons of tribulation, as Jemar Tisby notes, "Black Christianity in the United States grew alongside the explosive expansion of slavery and the hardening of racial boundaries in the United States. The faith of black Christians helped them endure and even inspired some believers to resist oppression."[7]

STEADY VOICES

Other Black voices in American history were not as vocal but were equally important—voices like my grandfather, who maintained a steady influence in the lives of his descendants, reminding them from where they had come.

Filmmaker and photographer Adrian L. Burrell does a wonderful job telling these stories. In 2020, he created a short film about his grandmother, Theresa Lewis, and the incredible impact she has had. She was born in Minden, Louisiana, grew up as an orphan, and did not remember her mama or daddy. She was raised by her aunts and uncles and lived in Louisiana till 1945. She spent her childhood moving from farm to farm and working in White people's homes, was married at thirteen, and had her first child that same year. After getting into a scuffle with one of the White farmers, Theresa's young husband knew it was time to flee the South. They packed up their few belongings and moved to Oakland, California.

Eventually, she bought a small, two-bedroom home for $5,000. Her first husband died at thirty-seven from an asthma attack.

Eventually, she remarried and found work in barbecue joints and card clubs and became known as the "Queen of San Pablo."

In the years of the war in Vietnam, the drug crisis, and gang activities in Oakland, Lewis was always there for her family. Today, moving and death have separated their family. She has 16 children, 58 grandchildren, 112 great-grandchildren, and 158 great-great-grandchildren. She's outlived both her husbands and buried nine of her kids.[8]

This left Burrell to observe, "I've been filming her for a while now. And I'll keep filming. The important part of this work probably won't happen for another 100 years or so. And I'm okay with that. Long after I'm gone, and even longer after my grandma, our people are going to have something to look back on. And that's enough for me."[9]

I resonate with stories like Theresa Lewis's, and they make me think of my own ancestors. I recall people such as Sojourner Truth, an abolitionist, activist, lecturer, and religious leader who became the first Black woman to speak out publicly against slavery; or Eartha White, a community leader who was Jacksonville's first Black social worker and census taker; or Fannie Coppin, who became the national president of the Women's Home and Foreign Missionary Society of the AME Church.

NONVIOLENT VOICE

Some voices in Black history have used their speech to justify violence. But MLK Jr.'s approach was different. He advocated a nonviolent approach, but as his late wife Coretta Scott King has often pointed out, he did so in an active rather than a passive manner. She made this observation around the turn of the twenty-first century:

> Both Gandhi and my husband understood that the great advantage of nonviolence is that its success does not

depend on the integrity of political leaders. It depends on the courage and commitment of people of goodwill. To meet the challenge of the Nobel laureates, we must join together in creating a nonviolent movement to achieve peace with justice that spans the globe. With courage and determination, we must sound the knell for the end of fear, apathy, and indifference to human suffering and proclaim a new century of hope, a century of protest and nonviolent resistance to injustice and repression throughout the nation and around the world.[10]

The nonviolent approach King took is summarized in his famous Six Principles of Nonviolence:

- Principle One: Nonviolence Is a Way of Life for Courageous People.

- Principle Two: Nonviolence Seeks to Win Friendship and Understanding.

- Principle Three: Nonviolence Seeks to Defeat Injustice, or Evil, Not People.

- Principle Four: Nonviolence Holds That Unearned, Voluntary Suffering for a Just Cause Can Educate and Transform People and Societies.

- Principle Five: Nonviolence Chooses Love Instead of Hate.

- Principle Six: Nonviolence Believes That the Universe Is on the Side of Justice.[11]

King saw a nonviolent approach as the most effective and active way to resist evil. And when he was murdered on April 4, 1968, much of what King embodied was carried on through the lives of people who followed his philosophy. Because of his commitment to speak up and be a nonviolent voice for change, even at the expense of his own life, a part of Black America was never the same. His vision for a global village where people

could be judged for the content of their character was passed
on to generation after generation. According to Cone, "For
King nonviolence was more than a strategy; it was the way of
life defined by love for others—the only way to heal broken
humanity. Hate created more hate and violence more violence.
King believed that the cycle of violence and hate could be
broken only with nonviolence and love, as revealed in Jesus'
rejection of violence and his acceptance of a shameful death on
a cruel cross."[12]

SAY SOMETHING

Unfortunately, the cancel culture era we live in today has made
it tougher for many to speak up. People weigh their options
and conclude that the price for saying something is too great,
so they remain silent. But here I must come back to the importance of becoming comfortable with being uncomfortable. Yes,
there may be times when you need to step back from the racial
justice conversation because the weight of it is too great. But
so long as you are able and it does not cause harm to your
physical well-being, you have an obligation to lean in when
times are difficult. This means that when you see an issue of
racial injustice, you speak up.

Sometimes our own biases wash over us in ways we did not
anticipate, and we need others to call us out. Such was the
case with the apostle Peter, the same Peter of whom Jesus
said, "On this rock I will build my church." He was a man who
loved Jesus, yet, in Galatians 2, the apostle Paul shares this
unflattering detail:

> When Cephas [Peter] came to Antioch, I opposed him to
> his face, because he stood condemned. For before certain
> men came from James, he used to eat with the Gentiles.
> But when they arrived, he began to draw back and

separate himself from the Gentiles because he was afraid of those who belonged to the circumcision group. The other Jews joined him in his hypocrisy, so that by their hypocrisy even Barnabas was led astray. (Galatians 2:11-13)

Because of Jesus' sacrifice we know that no one person is considered more important than any other person. Paul reminds us of this when he states that there is no such thing as Jew or Gentile. Christ tore down the wall that had divided these two groups of people when he died on the cross. Peter knew this and even acted on this belief. However, when the pressure mounted and he wanted to please certain Christian elites, he reverted to his old ways. Ironically, a humble fisherman who was literally offered a seat at the Lord's Table struggled to pass this same full blessing on to others. And in that moment, Paul could have remained silent. But if he had done so, much of the work Christ had begun in the lives of those earlier believers would have been undercut by two prominent church leaders with power. Instead, Paul recognized what was happening and spoke up. You and I are challenged to do the same.

In his "Letter from Birmingham Jail," King addresses the sentiment that we should sit silently and wait:

We know through painful experience that freedom is never voluntarily given by the oppressor; it must be demanded by the oppressed. Frankly, I have never yet engaged in a direct-action movement that was "well timed" according to the timetable of those who have not suffered unduly from the disease of segregation. For years now I have heard the word "wait." It rings in the ear of every Negro with a piercing familiarity. This "wait" has almost always meant "never." It has been a tranquilizing thalidomide, relieving the emotional stress for a moment, only to give birth to an ill-formed infant of frustration. We must come to see with the distinguished jurist of yesterday that "justice too long delayed is justice denied."[13]

King realized there came a point where it was imperative that he and others speak up because speaking up is also a part of standing with others in solidarity. Good thoughts must give way to concrete action. And as we take these steps, we must do so by embodying compassion. My life's verse is Matthew 9:36: "When [Jesus] saw the crowds, he had compassion on them, because they were harassed and helpless, like sheep without a shepherd." That phrase "he had compassion" (or "he was moved with compassion," as the old King James Version says) has come to my mind often and reminds me to show up with heart.

When we start to speak up and our hearts become engaged, our bond with people grows and we, too, are moved with compassion to stand up and do something.

SPEAKING INVOLVES ACTION

Speaking up always involves acting out in ways that tangibly involve action. In contemporary terms, it's not enough to have a black tile on your Facebook profile picture or a Black Lives Matter bumper sticker on your car. Instead, you need to put what you know is true into action.

This is a theme I see repeated in so many scriptural accounts and it's why Jesus' half brother James says in James 2:26, "As the body without the spirit is dead, so faith without deeds is dead." You can believe or speak about something all you want, but there comes a time when you must put your words into action.

Few passages in Scripture illustrate this point better than Luke 5:18-26:

Some men came carrying a paralyzed man on a mat and tried to take him into the house to lay him before Jesus. When they could not find a way to do this because of the crowd, they went up on the roof and lowered him on his mat through the tiles into the middle of the crowd, right in front of Jesus.

When Jesus saw their faith, he said, "Friend, your sins are forgiven."

The Pharisees and the teachers of the law began thinking to themselves, "Who is this fellow who speaks blasphemy? Who can forgive sins but God alone?"

Jesus knew what they were thinking and asked, "Why are you thinking these things in your hearts? Which is easier: to say, 'Your sins are forgiven,' or to say, 'Get up and walk'? But I want you to know that the Son of Man has authority on earth to forgive sins." So he said to the paralyzed man, "I tell you, get up, take your mat and go home." Immediately he stood up in front of them, took what he had been lying on and went home praising God. 26 Everyone was amazed and gave praise to God. They were filled with awe and said, "We have seen remarkable things today."

The reason this encounter was so remarkable lies in both the power of Jesus and the faith of those who came to him. Unlike Job's friends, who spoke and pulled him down, these friends acted and carried their friend to Jesus, doing whatever it took to see him healed. This is what it means to break the silence. It involves supporting those around who are in need, even if doing so makes us stand out from the crowd and requires some personal sacrifice.

Speaking up means being an ally for others and taking a stand with others. The word *ally* comes from the Latin word *alligare*, which means "to bind to." Thus, when we speak up and become an ally for others, we are bound together with them in ways we were not previously. This is one of the reasons Paul instructed believers in Galatians 6:2 to "carry each other's burdens." It's as we bear the loads of others that we become who God means us to be.

This points us to the importance of community. As Christians, we were never intended to serve on our own individual islands. Instead, we were intended to live together in harmony, to lift one another up in a broken world, and to tear down any walls that would keep us apart.

APPLICATION

Have you ever been bullied, overlooked, or mistreated? How did you respond? Every day, people used their words to put you down. And as they did, no one said a word. Maybe other people saw this unfold and they were afraid that if they were the first to speak up, they would get into trouble and make life harder for themselves. And so they remained silent.

Did you have someone to speak up for you? Did they come to your defense and speak up for you, helping you emerge feeling safe, protected, and as though you belonged?

Lastly, were you the one who did the bullying because you knew there was no one to speak up on behalf of the person being bullied?

In any event, we can all attest that it is important for people to speak up against the mistreatment in society. Life is full of issues that have bullied people, oppressed people, and held people back because of historical implications. And when injustice occurs or we notice this type of bullying, we have one of two options. We can shrivel up under the weight of the discomfort, or we can speak up and stand for the oppressed.

Is there an area of injustice you see in your community today? If so, refuse to be silent anymore because silence is complicity. Use your voice where you have influence—in your place of work or ministry, on social media in a respectful way, or to people in positions of power to make a difference. Your voice and perspective could be used by God to shift perspectives and create a more just world.

BE
THE SOLUTION

Everyone has regrets, and one of these can be failing to act. Just as failing to invest in a retirement plan in our younger years can cause us to miss out on millions of dollars in our seventies, failing to invest adequately in relationships can result in a life filled with regrets and devoid of the many friendships that could have been. There is always a ripple effect to our action or inaction, and we often miss out on opportunities in the moment because we do not consider the long-term benefits involved.

Think back to a time in your life when you could have made more of an effort to get to know someone. You could have kept in touch with that high school friend, spent more time with your kids while they were young, or gotten to know that coworker before he or she moved to another state. There might be a particular memory that haunts you. One where you could have stood up for someone who was bullied or was in pain, but you neglected to do something. You might not have had any ill intent, but your silence and inaction kept a friendship from developing or left a person to handle discrimination alone.

When it comes to racial injustice, it's easy to think, *This is an important topic, but I'm living a comfortable life. Why should I do anything to mess this up? What's in it for me if I do?* This mindset is why many people remain silent when it comes to matters of racial injustice. They want to see a "payoff" for their actions, and when they cannot see how their "selfless actions" benefit them, their company, or their reputation, they grow silent.

A few weeks before I was involved in that near-fatal car accident, I was at the Georgia State Capitol to represent Love Beyond Walls and our partnership with the Boyce L. Ansley School in downtown Atlanta.[1] This school serves forty-four K–12 students experiencing homelessness. All of the students are Black, and even though this school is small, I am proud we partnered with it and feel it is critical to leverage my platform in order to help these students have experiences such as touring the state capitol. As they get these opportunities, they see how power and privilege shape society's laws.

During the walkthrough, a local reporter asked me why I was so excited to help these kids have this opportunity. "Because I never had a chance to do this," I responded. "No one taught me how politics shaped social life." In fact, it wasn't until much later in life that I had any type of opportunity like these kids were experiencing that day. I didn't want these innocent children to miss out on opportunities just because they were unseen. I knew this experience could inspire some of them to have careers in the very building in which they stood.

There were so many ways my heart resonated with these kids. Like them, I knew what it was like to be a Black male, have experiences with homelessness as a teenager, be overlooked and mistreated. And I've seen how my experiences have given me the opportunity to leverage my background to help others in need today.

When it comes to racial injustice, we need people who are willing to step forward and say, "Hey, I never had this opportunity when I was a kid, and I want to help others who are discriminated against to have opportunities I never had." Likewise, we need those who have experienced tremendous privilege to recognize how much they have and to leverage their time, energy, and resources to help others who do not have these same benefits.

Together, we can have a tremendous impact as we confront history and present-day injustices.

STOP THEORIZING, START DOING

I am an avid reader. In my office are stacks of books I've devoured. I'm now in the process of completing a PhD in public policy and social change. As part of this education journey, I worked on a literature review and read the works of numerous authors on my chosen topic. But the problem I have is that as soon as I get started on this process, I don't know where to stop. I finish one book, see the bibliography at the end, and instantly want to read all the other cited sources. Knowledge is good, and I've been so blessed with the many writers and communicators I've never known who have spoken truth into my life.

But the challenge I face is one we all wrestle with when it comes to the subject of knowledge. What do we do with what we've learned? I've known some people who seem to love knowledge for knowledge's sake. They like being able to sit at cocktail parties and share the latest books they've read and discuss the ways their mindset has evolved. When I was part of a pastor's network in Atlanta, the White pastors in our group spoke about the White pastors they listened to.

Knowledge is good. But too much knowledge with too little application can make learners proud and cause them to view understanding as the end of their journey without ever putting their knowledge into action.

In the aftermath of George Floyd's murder, many people on social media posted black tiles to represent the life that had been snuffed out. This was good and appropriate to raise awareness for some, but for many it stopped there when they could have done so much more. Speaking out against racial injustice is one thing, but living a life marked by the rhythm of Jesus is another. The more we learn, the more we are obligated to act on what we know. The Scripture 1 John 1:7 tells us to "walk in the light, as he is in the light." What is light? It's knowledge. This means that as we learn, we are to put that learning into action through the way we live. We do not learn for the sake of acquiring more knowledge. We learn so we can better understand what it means to stand in solidarity with others and thus change the way we behave.

In short, we need fewer people to talk about solutions and more people to be the solution. We need less time spent on theorizing and more time spent on activism. It's easy to look at our broken world and say, "Wow, this is such a mess. What do we do from here?" But a better approach is to take a step back and ask, "How can I be a catalyst for change? How can I be the solution?"

GREAT FRIENDS AND GREAT VOICES

During the pandemic, I lost many people I thought were friends. As it turns out, speaking out on racial injustice came with a steep price, and I remember what it felt like to be cut off and have people in White spaces stop speaking to me or hold me at a distance. Only in retrospect have I recognized this as a form of trauma.

Even the process of writing this book was difficult. At various points, I found myself tense up; my palms would get sweaty as I relived some of my experiences. In one sense, I found this journey cathartic. But in another, it was difficult.

In *My Grandmother's Hands*, Resmaa Menakem writes about the racial trauma that can extend from generation to generation. As he describes, everyone deals with this trauma in different ways. He writes, "In today's America, we tend to think of healing as something binary: either we're broken or we're healed from that brokenness. But that's not how healing operates, and it's almost never how human growth works. More often, healing and growth take place on a continuum, with innumerable points between utter brokenness and total health."[2]

But along with the trauma and loss I experienced the solidi-fication of lifelong friendships. I think about my White friend Ellis Prince, a pastor in Baltimore who has been the leader of his church for almost ten years. Several times a month, Ellis will give me a call and allow me to lament and pray with him. He encourages me to vent my frustrations, grieve my losses, and share my fears. Or there's Kevin Dunlap who texted me prayers almost every Sunday, and Brian Bloye who would give me space to talk about the depths of the racial struggle.

My good friend Dr. Jerome Lubbe does the same. As a CEO and founder at Thrive Humancare, and as someone who has a background in social emotional well-being, Jerome often comes over to my house (apart from my injury), sits on my deck, and lets me share some of the trauma I am experiencing. I've been able to speak with him about the many hate messages that have come my way and the injustices I have faced. Having White allies in my life like Ellis, Kevin, Brian, Jerome, and others is incredibly life giving. And it's a constant reminder that not everyone who has a different skin color is in opposition to me.

The pandemic exposed a lot of racial division that many people thought was not there. Even churches that thought they had made a lot of progress realized how far they needed to go. But during this season, I was always reminded of my White and BIPOC friends like Jemar Tisby, Tyler Burns, Dominique Gilliard, Daniel Hill, Helen Lee Brooks, Lisa Sharon Harper, Marla Tavian, Nancy Wang Yuen, Oh Happy Dani, Ekemini Uwan, and others who continue to speak out and help people of all races to understand better how we can come together to fight systemic injustice. Their voices and others remind me of how important people of all backgrounds can be to this conversation.

DO SOMETHING

I close with these words of Jesus:

> The apostles gathered around Jesus and reported to him all they had done and taught. Then, because so many people were coming and going that they did not even have a chance to eat, he said to them, "Come with me by yourselves to a quiet place and get some rest." So they went away by themselves in a boat to a solitary place. But many who saw them leaving recognized them and ran on foot from all the towns and got there ahead of them. When Jesus landed and saw a large crowd, he had compassion on them, because they were like sheep without a shepherd. So he began teaching them many things. By this time it was late in the day, so his disciples came to him. "This is a remote place," they said, "and it's already very late. Send the people away so that they can go to the surrounding countryside and villages and buy themselves

something to eat." But he answered, "You give them something to eat." (Mark 6:30-37)

Those last six words always get me: "You give them something to eat." In other words, "Don't just tell everyone to go home and say you've done the best you can. Do something yourself."

Similarly, sometimes racial injustice in America can stare at us like a crowd of thousands of people who are hungry for bread of acceptance and belonging. And it's tempting to take one look at the situation and say, "Hey, there's nothing I can do because the need is too great." But in these moments, it's important to pause and do for one person what we wish we could do for everyone. It's being like Jesus, willing to go after that one lost sheep and search for that one lost coin.

Small actions, such as reaching out to someone of color and learning their story, might not appear to do much to save the world. But for you and for the person you serve, they can have an enormous impact. And so today, do for one person what you wish you could do for everyone. I leave you with two important words: *do something*.

AFTERWORD

We don't have to stay here.

As I read Terence Lester's *All God's Children*, the words "we don't have to stay here" leaped into my mind and communed with me because we don't. As God said to the people of Israel in Deuteronomy 1:6, "You have stayed long enough at this mountain."

Haven't we, family? Haven't we been where we are, grappling with understanding and embracing our interconnectedness in God, long enough? Haven't we been fragmented and dehumanized by racism long enough? Haven't we turned away from authentic repentance for sins of the past, which birthed the injustices of the present, long enough?

The painful truth is that we never had to be here, and the very lengthy stay here has cost lives, communities, culture, and our ability to see each other's humanity. The hopeful truth is we can move away from where we have been and on and up to brighter days. But it starts with us.

My dear brother's book is an invitation to be a part of that movement, a movement that requires us all to stand in solidarity with one another. Terence's words here are filled with light and beckon us to see the divine in each other, evolve beyond the biases we've learned, not fear history, truly hear each other's stories, and rejoice in the fact that we all belong to God and belong with each other.

So here we are with this invitation in hand, grappling with these issues and knowing that if we stand open to receive a new way of showing up in the world, God can pierce our hearts and minds and lead us in a new direction.

What will our response be? Will we stay where we are, refusing to reckon with the past in a way that allows for a love-filled future? Will we close our ears to stories that juxtapose the often-graceless traditions that we have accepted without questioning? Why not do a new thing? What's beyond our comfort? What's much more God-like than religion?

The answer is belonging.

If we accept this invitation, we are telling God that we want to acknowledge and experience belonging. We are expressing that we desire the shift from putrid passion for divisions and disparities based on nation, gender, race, and religion to a compassionate determination to cultivate belonging for everyone. There is enough room in God's beloved community for all to dwell there.

Now, I know someone reading this may be thinking, *We're not supposed to belong. If we're "Christian," we are to be "in the world, not of the world."*

I'm concerned that many have misunderstood these words. They are not telling us to disconnect from each other, but to have a Christlike perspective concerning each other and Christlike love for each other. Why would we, who are made in the image of God and placed on earth together, be then commissioned by the One who came for all to not be for each other?

We belong in God. We belong with each other. And somehow, as Dr. Martin Luther King Jr. said, "We must learn to live together," or "we will perish together as fools."

Terence has provided us with some of the ways we can take this journey, and it is up to us to respond with open hearts. He has challenged us to carry the teachings here into our everyday lives and live like Christ.

He has called us to remember that "history impacts story," and that we should focus on justice and seek true reconciliation, which is not a "sorry" but a solidarity stance. He has also challenged us to break any routine that renders us limited or lifeless as a vessel for love, truth, and justice.

Finally, let's RSVP yes to Terence's invitation and show up by doing the following:

Let's unpack and understand our own stories, including our cultural dynamics.

Let's not center our stories when someone else is telling their story.

Let's examine how our stories are connected instead of how they are divided.

Let's release harmful biases and commit to not picking them up again.

Let's embrace grace and belonging for all.

Let's commit to being educated in our history, knowing what racism is and does, and being involved in healing for everyone.

Let's learn more about people's critical needs and the history of why they exist.

Let's help to meet the needs and stop the real reasons they exist, putting an end to the why.

Let's truly share the love that overcomes evil and casts out darkness because God is love.

Let's get in on the type of justice that brings God glory.

Let's all read this book again and again, and be reminded to stand in solidarity with one another.

Because we are *all God's children*.

ACKNOWLEDGMENTS

I remember receiving the call from my father, Tyrone Lester, that my grandfather had just been rushed to the hospital after falling in his house. I was out of town at the time and called my auntie on FaceTime after they got him stable to let him know that I loved him and that I hoped he had a quick recovery. Little did I know that the hospital visit would reveal that he had stage IV pancreatic cancer and would be moved to hospice at home.

Finding that out and going to see him in his last moments of life changed me deeply. I reflected on the moments when he would bring the family together for cookouts, work to get me out of trouble when I was a teenager, talk to me as a father when mine wasn't tangibly present, and tell me that family was the most important thing we have and always to honor the Lester name. Well, a part of this acknowledgment is honoring the Lester name by saying, "Papa, I will never forget the moments you impacted my life when I was a child. I love you, Herman Lester Sr., and I will always cherish you and Grannie, Jessica Lester."

In similar fashion, I would like to acknowledge my family and honor those I have met along the way who have become family. It is with humility and love that I acknowledge the people who are helping me to build upon what my grandfather and grandmother set forth over seventy years.

First, I'd like to acknowledge my wife, Cecilia Lester. When I was writing this book, I was going through some of the hardest moments in life, but you kept pushing me to write one more sentence. You are my inspiration and the reason I have never given up on my dreams. You are my rock and my best friend. Thank you for being my number-one encourager. I also thank and acknowledge my children, Zion Joy and Terence II, with similar gratitude. Zion, I am extremely excited about our collaboration with coauthoring our children's book, and Terence II, I am grateful to play basketball, fish, and dream with you of the businesses you say you want to run. Thank you for always making my days worth fighting through. You not only inspire me and push me to pave the way, but you remind me every day of the bright future you each have ahead of you.

I also would like to acknowledge my mother, Dr. Connie Walker, for encouraging me to keep chasing my PhD dreams; my sister, Ashley Lester, and my nephew Carmelo; and my father, Tyrone Lester, who has become a man that I admire and consider a close friend. I am grateful that God has allowed us to enjoy our talks and our bond in special ways. Many thanks, too, to my stepfather, Dewitt Walker Sr., for always giving me the talks I needed to forge forward on this journey. I consider you a father figure. I would like to acknowledge my grandparents, Carlton and Gloria York, for sowing the seeds of resilience and wisdom in my life. I would like to thank my sister, Monica Lester, who is a very close friend and encourager in my life. Thank you for getting me through some of my hardest days on the road to obtaining my PhD. I am so close to the time when there will be two Dr. Lesters.

I would like to acknowledge the late Artie Glenn Shaw and the entire Shaw family who had a huge impact on my life during my younger years. With similar gratitude I would like to thank my friend and brother Ali Brathwaite and his wife, Arlene, for always supporting our work with Love Beyond Walls through film.

I'd also like to thank my book agent, Tawny Johnson, who has become like family and who pushes me with each book. Thank you for seeing the possibility for and potential of a third book and for believing that my daughter and I could also offer the world wisdom in children's books.

Special thanks to my editor, Al Hsu. Thank you for always listening to my ideas when we are in person. I also thank you for believing in my work and encouraging me to continue to use my voice for change.

A special thank you to the whole IVP family. Thank you for believing in me, my voice, and allowing me to grow with you with each book you pick up. Thank you for welcoming me with open arms and for believing that BIPOC stories matter.

I'd like to thank two of my closest friends, Harvey Strickland and his wife, Takeisha Strickland, for walking with me and Cecilia, and for having such beautiful kids.

Thanks to the Love Beyond Walls team, every volunteer who has ever served and all those who have supported our advocacy work over the years. Thank you all for being a part of a movement of doers.

Thank you to my friend Daniel Hill. Thank you for writing the foreword to this book and seeing my words and work as something that is needed in this world.

Thank you all for supporting and following my writing journey, and I hope to see you in the next book. Hopefully, by the time you hold this book, it will be Dr. Lester. (See, Papa? The legacy lives on.)

APPENDIX

FURTHER EDUCATIONAL MATERIAL

Books to read
- *Where Do We Go from Here?* by Martin Luther King Jr.
- *Jesus & the Disinherited* by Howard Thurman
- *The Cross and the Lynching Tree* by James Cone
- *The New Jim Crow* by Michelle Alexander
- *Why Are All the Black Kids Sitting Together in the Cafeteria?* by Beverly Tatum
- *Just Mercy: A Story of Justice and Redemption* by Bryan Stevenson
- *The Hate You Give* by Angie Thomas
- *Between the World & Me* by Ta-Nehisi Coates
- *Go Tell It on the Mountain* by James Baldwin
- *Invisible Man* by Ralph Ellison
- *The Color of Compromise* by Jemar Tisby
- *Rethinking Mass Incarceration* by Dominique Gilliard
- *Reading While Black* by Esau McCaulley
- *Disability and the Church* by Lamar Hardwick
- *Young, Gifted, and Black* by Sheila Wise Rowe
- *Healing Racial Trauma* by Sheila Wise Rowe
- *Black Man in a White Coat* by Damon Tweedy
- *I'm Still Here* by Austin Channing Brown
- *The Souls of Black Folks* by W. E. B. Du Bois
- *April 4, 1968,* by Michael Eric Dyson

- *Beloved* by Toni Morrison
- *Stamped from the Beginning* by Dr. Ibram X. Kendi
- *How to Be an Antiracist* by Dr. Ibram X. Kendi
- *I Know Why the Caged Bird Sings* by Maya Angelou
- *Me and White Supremacy* by Layla F. Saad
- *Sister Outsider* by Audre Lorde
- *So You Want to Talk About Race* by Ijeoma Oluo
- *The Fire Next Time* by James Baldwin
- *The Warmth of Other Suns* by Isabel Wilkerson
- *Their Eyes Were Watching God* by Zora Neale Hurston

Films or TV series to watch

- *13th*
- *American Son*
- *Dear White People*
- *Fruitvale Station*
- *I Am Not Your Negro*
- *If Beale Street Could Talk*
- *Just Mercy*
- *King in the Wilderness*
- *Selma*
- *The Hate U Give*
- *When They See Us*
- *Judas and the Black Messiah*
- *Let It Fall: Los Angeles 1982–1992*
- *BlacKkKlansman*
- *Hidden Figures*
- *The Kalief Browder Story*
- *Do the Right Thing*
- *12 Years a Slave*

NOTES

INTRODUCTION: EVERYONE HAS A STORY

[1] Rev. Dr. William J. Barber II, "Why the Poor People's Campaign 2022 Matters," *The Nation*, June 21, 2022, www.thenation.com/article/society/poor-peoples-campaign-barber-2022.

[2] Patricia Hill Collins, "Intersections of Race, Class, Gender, and Nation: Some Implications for Black Family Studies," *Journal of Comparative Family Studies* 29, no. 1 (Spring 1998): 27.

[3] Jeffrey Olivet, Marc Dones, and Molly Richard, "The Intersection of Homelessness, Racism, and Mental Illness," in *Racism and Psychiatry: Contemporary Issues and Interventions*, Morgan M. Medloc et al., eds. (Totowa, NJ: Humana Cham, 2019), https://doi.org/10.1007/978-3-319-90197-8_4.

[4] Jemar Tisby, *How to Fight Racism* (Grand Rapids, MI: Zondervan, 2021), Kindle.

[5] When I mention "seeing" I am talking about seeing people in totality—including their history, their stories, and everything that makes that person who they are in the world. When I use the word "we" I speak about society as a collective and how it is easy for anyone in society to miss the opportunity to see other people who emerge from a different social location than they do.

[6] Siri Carpenter, "Sights Unseen," *Monitor on Psychology*, April 2001, www.apa.org/monitor/apr01/blindness.

[7] "To Be in a Rage, Almost All the Time," NPR, June 1, 2020, www.npr.org/2020/06/01/867153918/-to-be-in-a-rage-almost-all-the-time.

[8] David Gillborn, "Intersectionality, Critical Race Theory, and the Primacy of Racism: Race, Class, Gender, and Disability in Education," *Qualitative Inquiry* 21, no. 3 (March 2015): 284.

[9] King made these comments in 1956. See King Center, "Dr. King's Fundamental Philosophy of Nonviolence," accessed March 30, 2022, https://thekingcenter.org/about-tkc/the-king-philosophy.

[10] Barack Obama, "Remarks of President Barack Obama at Student Roundtable in Istanbul," National Archives and Records Administration, accessed October 28, 2022, https://obamawhitehouse.archives.gov/realitycheck/the-press-office /remarks-president-barack-obama-student-roundtable-istanbul.

[11] Sheila Wise Rowe, *Healing Racial Trauma: The Road to Resilience* (Downers Grove, IL: InterVarsity Press, 2020), 10.

[12] Christina Barland Edmondson and Chad Brennan, *Faithful Antiracism: Moving Past Talk to Systemic Change* (Downers Grove, IL: InterVarsity Press, 2022), Kindle.

1. A PAST I COULD NOT TOUCH

[1] I gave a talk at TEDx Collier Heights in September 2021 about parenting Black children.

[2] Pria Mahadevan, "'The Talk' Is a Rite of Passage in Black Families Even When the Parent Is a Police Officer," Georgia Public Broadcasting, June 26, 2020, www .gpb.org/news/2020/06/26/the-talk-rite-of-passage-in-black-families -even-when-the-parent-police-officer.

[3] Leslie A. Anderson, Margaret O'Brien Caughy, and Margaret T. Owen, "'The Talk' and Parenting While Black in America: Centering Race, Resistance, and Refuge," *Journal of Black Psychology* 48, no. 3-4 (July 2022), https://doi .org/10.1177/00957984211034294.

[4] Cheyanne M. Daniels, "Texas Board of Education Strikes Down Proposal to Call Slavery 'Involuntary Relocation,'" *The Hill,* July 1, 2022, https://thehill.com /homenews/state-watch/3544271-texas-board-of-education-strikes-down -proposal-to-call-slavery-involuntary-relocation.

[5] LaGarrett J. King, "When Lions Write History: Black History Textbooks, African-American Educators, & the Alternative Black Curriculum in Social Studies Education, 1890-1940," *Multicultural Education* 22, no. 1 (2014): 2-11.

[6] King, "When Lions Write History."

[7] Edward E. Baptist, *The Half Has Never Been Told: Slavery and the Making of American Capitalism* (New York: Basic Books, 2016), xxi.

[8] James W. Loewen, *Lies My Teacher Told Me: Everything Your American History Textbook Got Wrong* (New York: Atria Books, 2007), 85.

[9] "The Origins of Modern Day Policing," NAACP, December 3, 2021, https:// naacp.org/find-resources/history-explained/origins-modern-day-policing.

[10] "Carter G. Woodson," NAACP, Civil Rights Leaders, May 10, 2021, https:// naacp.org/find-resources/history-explained/civil-rights-leaders/carter -g-woodson.

[11] "Carter G. Woodson."

[12] Christina Barland Edmondson and Chad Brennan, *Faithful Antiracism: Moving Past Talk to Systemic Change* (Downers Grove, IL: InterVarsity Press, 2022), Kindle.

2. A HISTORY FEW WANTED TO UNDERSTAND

[1] Bobby Allyn and Tamara Keith, "Twitter Permanently Suspends Trump, Citing 'Risk of Further Incitement of Violence,'" NPR, January 8, 2021, www.npr .org/2021/01/08/954760928/twitter-bans-president-trump-citing-risk-of -further-incitement-of-violence.

[2] The Trump Twitter account was permanently suspended following tweets that caused major division. Recently, Twitter was purchased by Elon Musk, and Musk did an online Twitter poll that asked people if they thought he should reinstate Trump's account. The vote leaned in favor of the restoration of Trump's Twitter account, and Elon Musk has since restored it.

[3] Andrea González-Ramírez, "The Ever-Growing List of Trump's Most Racist Rants," *GEN*, June 22, 2020, https://gen.medium.com/trump-keeps-saying -racist-things-heres-the-ever-growing-list-of-examples-21774f6749a4.

[4] "CNN's Van Jones Brought to Tears as Joe Biden Wins US Election," YouTube, November 7, 2020, www.youtube.com/watch?v=9eMoCW1Pq54&ab_channel =GuardianNews.

[5] Esau McCaulley, *Reading While Black: African American Biblical Interpretation as an Exercise in Hope* (Downers Grove, IL: InterVarsity Press, 2020), 112.

[6] Christina Barland Edmondson and Chad Brennan, *Faithful Antiracism: Moving Past Talk to Systemic Change* (Downers Grove, IL: InterVarsity Press, 2022), Kindle.

3. GOD IS JUSTICE

[1] Resmaa Menakem, *My Grandmother's Hands: Racialized Trauma and the Pathway to Mending Our Hearts and Bodies* (Las Vegas: Central Recovery Press, 2017).

[2] Jay Croft, "Philando Castile Shooting: Dashcam Video Shows Rapid Event," CNN, June 21, 2017, www.cnn.com/2017/06/20/us/philando-castile -shooting-dashcam/index.html.

[3] Some White churches do this in hopes that one Black person would speak for all Black people, and it is not healthy to put that type of pressure on one person of color. Additionally, no one BIPOC person can speak for the suffering of all BIPOC people. We can share the suffering through our lens, but people must understand that collective suffering also is experienced differently by those who are impacted.

[4]The pastor at that church had several other harmful incidents that eventually revealed his primary focus of growing the congregation at all costs; he would run over anyone in his way, and eventually he caused the whole congregation to leave.

[5]Mae Elise Cannon, *Social Justice Handbook: Small Steps to a Better World* (Downers Grove, IL: InterVarsity Press, 2009), 19-20.

[6]J. Philip Wogaman, "The Social Justice Perspective," in *Church, State, and Public Justice: Five Views*, ed. P. C. Kemeny (Downers Grove, IL: InterVarsity Press, 2007), 221.

[7]Henri Nouwen, *Turn My Mourning into Dancing* (Nashville: Thomas Nelson, 2004), 7.

[8]Jemar Tisby, *How to Fight Racism: Courageous Christianity and the Journey Toward Racial Justice* (Grand Rapids, MI: Zondervan, 2021), 89.

[9]"White Christians Have Become Even Less Motivated to Address Racial Injustice," Barna Group, September 15, 2020, www.barna.com/research /american-christians-race-problem.

[10]Howard Thurman, *Jesus and the Disinherited* (Boston: Beacon Press, 1996).

[11]Terence Lester, "Why Racial Justice Is Distinctly Different Than Racial Reconciliation. And Why It Matters," *Christian Post*, February 24, 2021, www .christianpost.com/voices/why-racial-justice-is-different-than-racial -reconciliation.html.

[12]Bernice King (@BerniceKing), "Kindness matters," Twitter, February 3, 2021, 10:12 a.m., https://twitter.com/berniceking/status/135699910032407 7570?lang=en.

[13]James H. Cone, *The Cross and the Lynching Tree* (Maryknoll, NY: Orbis, 2011), 17.

[14]Gregory Coles, *Single, Gay, Christian: A Personal Journey of Faith and Sexual Identity* (Downers Grove, IL: InterVarsity Press, 2017), 70.

[15]Dainius, "Removed: Photographer Removes Phones from His Photos to Show How Terribly Addicted We've Become," Bored Panda, January 1, 2016, www .boredpanda.com/portraits-holding-devices-removed-eric-pickersgill/?utm _source=google&utm_medium=organic&utm_campaign=organic.

[16]Lester, "Why Racial Justice."

[17]This list is nowhere near exhaustive. These are books that shaped me in ways that gave me a better understanding on the Black experience. I have included a more robust list of books and films in the appendix of this book.

4. CONFRONTING BURIED HISTORY

[1]John Onwuchekwa, "4 Reasons We Left the SBC," The Front Porch, July 9, 2020, https://thefrontporch.org/2020/07/4-reasons-we-left-the-sbc.

[2] Maina Mwaura, "Atlanta Church Splits with SBC for Downplaying Racial Issues," *Christianity Today,* July 16, 2020, www.christianitytoday.com/news /2020/july/john-onwuchekwa-leave-sbc-african-american-atlanta-church .html.

[3] Jeffery Robinson, "History of Racism, Part I," King County TV, December 5, 2017, educational video, 2:30, www.youtube.com/watch?v=0-AxOROms0A &t=2067s&ab_channel=KingCountyTV.

[4] Chase Hutchinson, "An Interview with Lawyer Jeff Robinson About *Who We Are,* His New Documentary on Racism in America," *Portland Mercury Blog,* February 11, 2022, www.portlandmercury.com/blogtown/2022/02/11 /38410420/an-interview-with-lawyer-jeff-robinson-about-who-we-are -his-new-documentary-on-racism-in-america.

[5] Tracy Jan and Jose A. DelReal, "Carson Compares Slaves to Immigrants Coming to 'a Land of Dreams and Opportunity,'" *Washington Post,* March 6, 2017, www .washingtonpost.com/news/wonk/wp/2017/03/06/carson-compares-slaves -to-immigrants-coming-to-a-land-of-dreams-and-opportunity.

[6] Christopher Wilson, "Where's the Debate on Francis Scott Key's Slave-Holding Legacy?," *Smithsonian Magazine,* July 1, 2016, www.smithsonianmag.com /smithsonian-institution/wheres-debate-francis-scott-keys-slave-holding -legacy-180959550.

[7] Jemar Tisby, *The Color of Compromise: The Truth About the American Church's Complicity in Racism* (Grand Rapids, MI: Zondervan, 2019), 207.

[8] Alexander H. Stephens, "Cornerstone Speech," American Battlefield Trust, accessed November 23, 2022, www.battlefields.org/learn/primary-sources /cornerstone-speech.

[9] Abraham Lincoln, "Address on Colonization to a Deputation of Negroes," August 14, 1862, in *Collected Works of Abraham Lincoln,* vol. 5 (Ann Arbor: University of Michigan Digital Library Production Services, 2001), 375, https://quod.lib.umich.edu/l/lincoln/lincoln5/1:812?rgn=div1;view=full text.

[10] Robinson, "History of Racism, Part I."

[11] Michelle Alexander, *The New Jim Crow: Mass Incarceration in the Age of Colorblindness* (New York: New Press, 2020), 37

[12] James H. Cone, *The Cross and the Lynching Tree* (Maryknoll, NY: Orbis, 2011), 26.

[13] Alexander, *The New Jim Crow,* 38.

[14] Isabel Wilkerson, *Caste: The Origins of Our Discontents* (New York: Random House, 2020), 133.

[15] Tisby, *Color of Compromise*, 105.

[16] Austin Channing Brown, *I'm Still Here: Black Dignity in a World Made for Whiteness* (New York: Crown, 2018), 116.

[17] Frank Brown, "Nixon's 'Southern Strategy' and Forces against Brown," *Journal of Negro Education* 73, no. 3 (Summer 2004): 191-208.

[18] Martin Luther King Jr., "Timeless Words from Martin Luther King Jr.," *Seattle Times*, January 19, 1998, https://archive.seattletimes.com/archive/?date=19980 119&slug=2729540.

[19] Eddie S. Glaude Jr., *Democracy in Black* (New York: Crown, 2016), 57.

5. UNPACKING BIASES

[1] Love Beyond Walls, "A Traveling Museum That Shares the Stories of Those Who Are Forgotten," www.lovebeyondwalls.org/dignity-museum.

[2] Anthony F. Casey, *Peoples on the Move: Community Research for Ministry and Missions* (Eugene, OR: Wipf & Stock, 2020), 34.

[3] Casey, *Peoples on the Move*, 40.

[4] Patricia Hill Collins, *On Intellectual Activism* (Philadelphia: Temple University Press, 2012).

[5] Omer Azriel and Yair Bar-Haim, "Attention Bias," in *Clinical Handbook of Fear and Anxiety: Maintenance Processes and Treatment Mechanisms*, ed. Jonathan S. Abramowitz and Shannon M. Blakey (Washington, DC: American Psychological Association, 2020), 203-18, https://doi.org/10.1037/0000150-012.

[6] Chimamanda Ngozi Adichie, "The Danger of a Single Story," www.youtube.com /watch?v=D9Ihs241zeg&ab_channel=TED.

[7] Cory Booker, "Cory Booker Gets Emotional Over Ketanji Brown Jackson's Nomination," March 24, 2022, www.youtube.com/watch?v=v8NiPzEJ4po&ab _channel=ABCNews.

[8] Dallas Willard, *Renovation of the Heart: Putting on the Character of Christ* (Colorado Springs: NavPress, 2002), 16.

[9] Colleen Walsh, "Historian Puts the Push to Remove Confederate Statues in Context," *Harvard Gazette*, June 19, 2020, https://news.harvard.edu/gazette /story/2020/06/historian-puts-the-push-to-remove-confederate-statues-in-context.

[10] Carlie Porterfield, "Virginia Tears Down Richmond's Robert E. Lee Statue, the Largest Confederate Monument in the U.S.," *Forbes*, September 8, 2021, www .forbes.com/sites/carlieporterfield/2021/09/08/virginia-tears-down -richmonds-robert-e-lee-statue-the-largest-confederate-monument-in-the -us/?sh=724639ad388f.

[11] Walsh, "Historian Puts the Push."

[12] Robert Monson (@RobertMonson), "Being an 'Ally' to Black People Must Transcend the Latest News Cycle. I Think Often of the Fervor of People in 2020 to Come to Our Rescue, Throw a Few Dollars, Read That One Book on Not Being Fragile, and Black out Squares . . . Did Those Things Continue? Fatigue Set in for Many," Twitter, August 30, 2022, https://twitter.com/robertjmonson/status/1564571832971304962?s=46&t=q6V4j4qUei7DVO-RxLIT5w.

6. ENGAGING DIFFERENCES

[1] My daughter saying that she was not Muslim was in no way attempting to insult Muslims. We respect and honor our Muslim brothers and sisters. However, my daughter is clear that she is Christian, and a White woman was attempting to use a derogatory remark about Muslims to discourage her and demonize Muslims.

[2] Eman Bare, "Head Wraps Aren't Just a NYFW Accessory," *Teen Vogue*, September 15, 2017, www.teenvogue.com/gallery/head-wraps-nyfw-history-cultural-appropriation.

[3] Through steps such as the Crown Act (which stands for Create a Respectful and Open World for Natural Hair), organizations were compelled to stop discriminating against Black women based on hair.

[4] Deepa Shivaram, "A Year Later, Atlanta Remembers the 8 People Killed in Spa Shootings," NPR, March 12, 2022, www.npr.org/2022/03/12/1086306008/atlanta-spa-shootings-anniversary-anti-asian-racism.

[5] *The Chinese Exclusion Act*, directed by Ric Burns and Li-Shin Yu, American Experience, PBS, 2018.

[6] Figure 1 is adapted from "Schema integration inclusion exclusion separation" illustration, Zerbor, Dreamstime.com.

[7] Sarah Pulliam Bailey, "Q&A: Rapper Lecrae on His Discomfort with Hearing Slavery Described as a 'White Blessing,'" *Washington Post*, June 16, 2020, www.washingtonpost.com/religion/2020/06/16/qa-rapper-lecrae-his-discomfort-with-hearing-slavery-described-white-blessing.

[8] Cornel West, *Race Matters* (New York: Vintage Books, 1994), 102.

[9] Michael Emerson, "Michael Emerson on Race and the Church," YouTube, 4:16, www.youtube.com/watch?v=T0Bgq6VlPCw&ab_channel=HenryCenter.

[10] Beverly Daniel Tatum, *Why Are All the Black Kids Sitting Together in the Cafeteria? And Other Conversations About Race* (New York: Basic Books, 2017), 114.

[11] Martin Luther King Jr., *Where Do We Go from Here: Chaos or Community?*, King Legacy Book 2 (Boston: Beacon Press, 2009), 74.

12 Havi Carel and Gita Györffy, "Seen but Not Heard: Children and Epistemic Injustice," *Lancet* 384, no. 9950 (October 4, 2014): 1256-57, https://doi.org/10.1016/S0140-6736(14)61759-1.

13 Helen Turnbull, "Assimilation: Hidden in Plain Sight: The Illusion of Inclusion—Part IV," *Diversity Journal*, July 31, 2014, https://diversityjournal.com/13988-assimilation-hidden-plain-sight.

14 Sydnee Crews, "It's Okay; You're One of Us," Medium, July 16, 2020. https://medium.com/@sydnee.crews/its-okay-you-re-one-of-us-d0904b79ef71.

15 "Florida City Hopes 'Baby Shark' Song Will Drive Homeless from Park," ABC Action News, July 17, 2019, www.youtube.com/watch?v=AR8eL0xMGpc&ab_channel=InsideEdition.

8. PRACTICE PROXIMITY

1 "Critical Race Theory FAQ," NAACP Legal Defense and Educational Fund, April 21, 2022, www.naacpldf.org/critical-race-theory-faq/?gclid=EAIaIQobChMIjejW9_za9wIVU8qzCh3VtwysEAAYAyAAEgLr9fD_BwE.

2 "Florida Rejects Publishers' Attempts to Indoctrinate Students," Florida Department of Education, April 15, 2022, www.fldoe.org/newsroom/latest-news/florida-rejects-publishers-attempts-to-indoctrinate-students.stml.

3 "Florida Rejects," Florida Department of Education.

4 James H. Cone, *The Cross and the Lynching Tree* (Maryknoll, NY: Orbis Books, 2011), 3-4.

5 Cone, *The Cross and the Lynching Tree*, 9.

6 James S. Damico and Ted Hall, "The Cross and the Lynching Tree: Exploring Religion and Race in the Elementary Classroom," *Language Arts* 92, no. 3 (2015): 187-98.

7 Love Beyond Walls, *Voiceless: A Documentary on Systemic Poverty*, https://vimeo.com/222830083.

8 Terence Lester, *When We Stand* (Downers Grove, IL: InterVarsity Press, 2021), 25.

9 Lester, *When We Stand*.

10 See William Barber on Roland S. Martin, "Rev. William Barber Delivers Masterful History Lesson, Declares 'It's Movement Time Again,'" YouTube video, 8:45, February 8, 2018, www.youtube.com/watch?v=CQzZowezRM4&ab_channel=RolandS.Martin.

11 William J. Barber II, "David George," in *Four Hundred Souls: A Community History of African America, 1619–2019*, ed. Ibram X. Kendi and Keisha N. Blain (New York: One World, 2021).

[12] William J. Barber II, *Forward Together: A Moral Message for the Nation*, (St. Louis, MO: Chalice Press, 2014), 113.

[13] Felicia Wu Song, *Restless Devices: Recovering Personhood, Presence, and Place in a Digital Age* (Downers Grove, IL: IVP Academic, 2021), 182.

[14] Lester, *When We Stand*, 10.

[15] Tracy Jan, "News Media Offers Consistently Warped Portrayals of Black Families, Study Finds," *Washington Post*, December 13, 2017, www.washington post.com/news/wonk/wp/2017/12/13/news-media-offers-consistently -warped-portrayals-of-black-families-study-finds.

[16] Travis L. Dixon, "A Dangerous Distortion of Our Families," Color of Change, January 2018, https://colorofchange.org/dangerousdistortion.

[17] William Barber on Roland S. Martin, "Rev. William Barber Delivers Masterful History Lesson," YouTube video, 25:40, www.youtube.com/watch?v=CQzZ owezRM4&ab_channel=RolandS.Martin.

9. SIT AT ANOTHER'S TABLE

[1] Martin Luther King Jr., "The Other America," speech delivered at Grosse Pointe High School in Michigan on March 14, 1968, www.gphistorical.org/mlk /mlkspeech.

[2] Derald Wing Sue, Christina M. Capodilupo, Gina C. Torino, Jennifer M. Bucceri, Aisha M. B. Holder, Kevin L. Nadal, and Marta Esquilin, "Racial Microaggressions in Everyday Life: Implications for Clinical Practice," *American Psychologist* 62, no. 4 (May-June 2007): 271-86, https://doi.org/10.1037/0003 -066X.62.4.271.

[3] Bernice King (@BerniceKing), "Even the Statement, 'Let's Invite More Black People to the Table,' Implies Ownership of the Table and Control of Who Is Invited. Racism Is About Power," Twitter, June 17, 2020, https://twitter.com /BerniceKing/status/1273105155970535424.

[4] Rev. Gricel Medina (@pastorgricel), "This Is a Very Painful Reality for Brown and Black Leaders. If the Table Is Owned by White and the Authority Voices Are White, Then We Are Nothing More than Tokens. If Our Voices Are Only Present to Empower Them . . . No Thank You!" Twitter, June 17, 2020, https:// twitter.com/pastorgricel/status/1273301158241751045.

[5] Ayana Archie, "2 Former Coaches Join Brian Flores in His Discrimination Suit Against the NFL," NPR, April 8, 2022, www.npr.org/2022/04/08/1091559405 /coaches-join-nfl-discrimination-lawsuit.

[6] As of August 2022, Condolezza Rice, Mellody Hobson, and Lewis Hamilton are limited partners in the group that owns the Denver Broncos. Arnie Stapleton, "Broncos Sport NFL's Richest, Most Diverse Ownership Group," U.S.News,

August 11, 2022, www.usnews.com/news/sports/articles/2022-08-11/broncos-sport-nfls-richest-most-diverse-ownership-group.

[7] Diane Langberg, Twitter post, April 8, 2021, https://mobile.twitter.com/DianeLangberg/status/1380188901365665794.

[8] Howard Thurman, *Jesus and the Disinherited* (Boston: Beacon Press, 1996), 88.

[9] Austin Channing Brown, *I'm Still Here: Black Dignity in a World Made for Whiteness* (New York: Crown, 2018), 169.

[10] Johnathan Alvarado, Facebook post, April 8, 2021, www.facebook.com/johnathan.alvarado.3/posts/pfbid066LMg76X3ijrW8TmFThSjBLjVbSzsbUbUsT6a1MjRVSLz8zA43YYhK72rG3BsfNNl.

[11] Mary-Frances Winters, *Black Fatigue: How Racism Erodes the Mind, Body, and Spirit* (Oakland, CA: Berrett-Koehler Publishers, 2020).

[12] Lamar Hardwick, *Disability and the Church: A Vision for Diversity and Inclusion* (Downers Grove, IL: InterVarsity Press, 2021), 33.

[13] "Edgar Chandler (Minister)," Wikipedia, Wikimedia Foundation, August 9, 2022, https://en.wikipedia.org/wiki/Edgar_Chandler_(minister).

[14] Krissah Thompson, "In March on Washington, White Activists Were Largely Overlooked but Strategically Essential" *Washington Post*, August 25, 2013, www.washingtonpost.com/lifestyle/style/in-march-on-washington-white-activists-were-largely-overlooked-but-strategically-essential/2013/08/25/f2738c2a-eb27-11e2-8023-b7f07811d98e_story.html.

[15] "NAACP," Wikipedia, Wikimedia Foundation, November 9, 2022, https://en.wikipedia.org/wiki/NAACP.

[16] Elizabeth Denevi and Lori Cohen, "White Antiracist Activists," Teaching While White, www.teachingwhilewhite.org/resources/white-antiracist-activists.

[17] Maura Hohman, "This 'Mister Rogers' Moment Broke Race Barriers. It's Just as Powerful Today," TODAY, June 8, 2020, www.today.com/popculture/how-mister-rogers-pool-moment-broke-race-barriers-t183635.

[18] Denevi and Cohen, "White Antiracist Activists."

[19] Rabbi Abraham Joshua Heschel, "Religion and Race," Black Past, March 21, 1965, www.blackpast.org/african-american-history/1963-rabbi-abraham-joshua-heschel-religion-and-race.

[20] See "Meet Dr. Jerome," Dr. Jerome, Patient-Doctor, accessed January 17, 2023, www.drjerome.com/about.

10. BREAK THE SILENCE

[1] Tajma Hall, "After More Than 100 Years of Attempts, Lynching Is Now a Federal Hate Crime," CBS58 News, March 30, 2022, www.cbs58.com/news/after-more-than-100-years-of-attempts-lynching-is-now-a-federal-hate-crime.

[2] "The National Memorial for Peace and Justice," Museum and Memorial, https:// museumandmemorial.eji.org/memorial.

[3] "August 28, 1955: Emmett Till Is Murdered," History Channel, This Day in History, www.history.com/this-day-in-history/the-death-of-emmett-till.

[4] "Montgomery Bus Boycott," History Channel, January 12, 2022, www.history .com/topics/black-history/montgomery-bus-boycott.

[5] "The Black Church: Black Jesus and Christianity," YouTube, March 31, 2021, www.youtube.com/watch?v=QdBhjtLtuDw&ab_channel=PBS, 1:56.

[6] James H. Cone, *The Cross and the Lynching Tree* (Maryknoll, NY: Orbis, 2011), 175.

[7] Jemar Tisby, *The Color of Compromise: The Truth About the American Church's Complicity in Racism* (Grand Rapids, MI: Zondervan, 2019), 57.

[8] Adrian L. Burrell, "My Grandma's Life, from Jim Crow Louisiana to Oakland," *Pop-Up Magazine*, www.youtube.com/watch?v=RaDkk3nFFDA&ab_channel =Pop-UpMagazine.

[9] Burrell, "My Grandma's Life."

[10] Coretta Scott King, "Coretta Scott King Reflects on Working Toward Peace," Architects of Peace, www.scu.edu/mcae/architects-of-peace/King/essay.html.

[11] King Center, "Dr. King's Fundamental Philosophy of Nonviolence."

[12] Cone, *The Cross and the Lynching Tree*, 125.

[13] Available online at www.csuchico.edu/iege/_assets/documents/susi-letter -from-birmingham-jail.pdf.

CONCLUSION: BE THE SOLUTION

[1] Liza Lucas, "Tuition-Free Atlanta School Focused on Helping Kids Experiencing Homelessness," 11 Alive, April 29, 2022, www.11alive.com/article/news/local /the-ansley-school-tuition-free-students-experiencing-homelessness/85-c13 e979b-c79a-4856-b8c5-c792812d26b6.

[2] Resmaa Menakem, *My Grandmother's Hands: Racialized Trauma and the Pathway to Mending Our Hearts and Bodies* (Las Vegas: Central Recovery Press, 2017).

ABOUT THE AUTHOR

Terence Lester is the founder and executive director of Love Beyond Walls. He is a storyteller, public scholar, speaker, community activist, and author. He believes that all people deserve equity, love, and a chance to change their lives. Terence is known for nationwide campaigns that bring awareness to issues surrounding homelessness, poverty, and economic inequality. His awareness campaigns on behalf of the poor have been featured on MLK50, CNN, *Good Morning America*, in *Essence Magazine* and *USA Today*, and have been viewed by millions of people worldwide. His greatest passion involves educating the general public about pressing issues that plague the lives of those who are vulnerable and voiceless and using the educational piece to mobilize an army of people to love and serve those who are unseen. Terence holds four degrees, is a current PhD candidate, and is the author of *I See You* and *When We Stand*. He is happily married to Cecilia, and together they have two wonderful children, Zion Joy and Terence II.

terencelester.com
twitter.com/imterencelester
facebook.com/imterencelester
instagram.com/imterencelester

ALSO BY TERENCE LESTER

When We Stand
978-0-8308-3178-4

I See You
978-0-8308-4572-9

ABOUT LOVE BEYOND WALLS

Love Beyond Walls is a movement birthed out of the hope that love is greater than walls. One of the most distinguishable characteristics of our organization is our focus on telling the stories of the unseen. We are committed to people that the world passes by because we believe the people struggling with poverty and sleeping on the streets have lives and stories that are just as valuable as ours.

We exist to provide dignity to the unhoused and poor by providing a voice, visibility, shelter, community, grooming, and support services to achieve self-sufficiency.

Address: 3270 East Main Street, College Park, GA 30337
Email: info@lovebeyondwalls.org
lovebeyondwalls.org
twitter.com/lovebeyondwalls
facebook.com/lovebeyondwalls
vimeo.com/lovebeyondwalls
instagram.com/lovebeyondwalls